Winning

with

Transglobal Leadership

How to Find and Develop Top Global Talent
to Build World-Class Organizations

Linda D. Sharkey, PhD
Nazneen Razi, PhD
Robert A. Cooke, PhD
Peter A. Barge

NEW YORK   CHICAGO   SAN FRANCISCO
LISBON   LONDON   MADRID   MEXICO CITY   MILAN
NEW DELHI   SAN JUAN   SEOUL   SINGAPORE
SYDNEY   TORONTO

The *McGraw·Hill* Companies

1 2 3 4 5 6 7 8 9 0   DOC/DOC   1 8 7 6 5 4 3 2

ISBN: 978-0-07-179051-2
MHID: 0-07-179051-9

e-ISBN: 978-0-07-179052-9
e-MHID: 0-07-179052-7

This publication is designed to provide accurate and authoritative information in regard to the subject matter covered. It is sold with the understanding that neither the author nor the publisher is engaged in rendering legal, accounting, securities trading, or other professional services. If legal advice or other expert assistance is required, the services of a competent professional person should be sought.

—*From a Declaration of Principles Jointly Adopted by a Committee of the American Bar Association and a Committee of Publishers and Associations*

Library of Congress Cataloging-in-Publication Data
Winning with transglobal leadership : how to find and develop top global talent to build world-class organizations / by Linda D. Sharkey ... [et al.].
  p. cm.
  ISBN 978-0-07-179051-2 (alk. paper)—ISBN 0-07-179051-9 (alk. paper)
1. Executive ability. 2. Leadership. 3. Executives—Recruiting. 4. Employee retention. I. Sharkey, Linda.
  HD38.2.W557   2012
  658.4'092—dc23

                                                      2011048862

To my husband Tom for all the support and love he has given me through our wonderful life together. Without him and his belief in me, my life would not be so rich. And to my parents who instilled in me the thirst for learning and in particular learning about other cultures. They would be so proud of this accomplishment.

L. D. S.

To my family for their patience, love, and support over the years; my husband Sal for making everything seem worthwhile; my son Faiz for his delightful sense of humor; my son Sam for his cheerful disposition, his wife Julie, and their delightful children Kamran and Laila.

N. R.

To my wife Janet and daughters Cathleen, Heather, and Jessica for their ever-lasting love, interest, and support at home and at the office for seemingly never-ending projects like this one.

R. A. C.

To Kinchem Hegedus, my wife and the real writer in our family, for supporting me and a project that seemed never to end. To Billy and Shannon for letting their dad encroach on their time so that those very rich interviews with transglobal leaders could take place at many and varied times.

P. A. B.

Contents

PART II

THE NUTS AND BOLTS OF TRANSGLOBAL LEADERS: WHAT THEY DO, HOW THEY THINK, AND HOW THEY INTERACT WITH OTHERS TO BUILD SUSTAINABLE BUSINESSES

PART III

ASSESSING AND DEVELOPING YOUR TRANSGLOBAL LEADERSHIP CAPABILITIES

Foreword

I have spent my professional career studying and developing leaders. This experience has taught me that over the long run, the organizations that are most conscientious about the selection and development of leadership talent excel in their marketplaces. The challenge, however, is that leadership itself is not static. In other words, leaders must always be adaptive and ready to meet emerging challenges and trends. Each era demands something different from its leaders. That is why this book by Sharkey, Razi, Cooke, and Barge is so compelling. These authors recognize the critical demands facing today's leaders. They define what it takes for leaders to function effectively in an increasingly interconnected, complex, and global world.

I first met Linda Sharkey, the member of the writing team with whom I have personally worked, when she was the head of global executive development for GE Capital. We worked together to help GE leaders become more effective communicators by using stories to convey their missions, values, and direction. This use of stories, with its departure from corporate pitches, was a real turning point for many of these leaders. We then moved to work with the boards of the companies in which GE invested. We helped their directors create more cohesive and effective board practices and relationships. This was a powerful initiative that we took all over the world. It was through these experiences with Linda that I saw her passion for developing outstanding leaders and, in turn, outstanding organizations.

Linda is not alone in this passion. Her coauthor Nazneen Razi, having served as head of human resources at several global and multinational firms, has seen firsthand the impact of less effective global leaders on business performance. Nazneen's business travels have taken her to numerous European and Asian countries, where she has had the opportunity to work with and assess hundreds of leaders in diverse settings. The richness of these multicultural experiences led her to team up with Linda to work on this book.

Peter Barge, an exemplar of global leadership from Jones Lang LaSalle, has also been passionate about discovering what separates great global leaders from others. Peter's career has spanned three continents, which has provided him a broad perspective on the variance of global leadership capability. He has been recognized for building sustainable businesses in many emerging markets, and he has served on boards in Europe, the Middle East, Asia, and Australia. Nazneen, Peter, and Linda joined together in their quest to discover what distinguished great global leaders from others. They sought to answer the fundamental question of why some succeeded while others failed so miserably.

Through their initial research, Linda, Nazneen, and Peter saw the need for a new survey and measurement framework to assess and develop global leaders. This led them to Rob Cooke, an expert in measurement whose surveys have been used extensively by leaders around the world. Rob's culture and leadership inventories, translated into over 20 languages and used in thousands of organizations, provided the foundation needed to move the book in a quantitative direction. The authors' partnership and variety of perspectives and backgrounds make for an important and timely book.

Their five behavioral dimensions of transglobal leaders have taken the thinking about what is required to succeed globally to a more sophisticated level. Their Transglobal Leadership Matrix is very insightful yet pragmatic, as well as easy to understand and apply. Any company playing in the global arena will benefit from this book, and any leader who needs to function more effectively globally will need to read this book.

Kudos to Linda, Nazneen, Rob, and Peter for their significant contribution to the leadership development field. This is a wonderful resource for leaders and their organizations. This book will make a difference in a world in need of global leaders.

Jay A. Conger
Los Angeles, California
Kravis Professor of Leadership Studies
Chairman, Kravis Leadership Institute
Claremont McKenna College

Acknowledgments

Linda D. Sharkey

- Sarah McArthur whose calm and professionalism helped take our book to the next level

- To Executive Network members with whom we tested our ideas and got great feedback and support to continue the project

- To all the great leaders that participated in the survey and who shared their stories and experiences that make this book so rich

- To all the great leaders that we have worked with over the years that formed the basis for why we should embark on this project and ultimately write the book

- To my fellow authors for their humor and perseverance through what seemed like a never-ending effort

Nazneen Razi

My deepest gratitude to:

- Jones Lang LaSalle for providing the context and landscape for testing the concepts; particularly, the transglobal leaders Colin Dyer, Lauralee Martin, Alastair Hughes, and Christian Ulbrich

- All the transglobal leaders for sharing their experiences and making this a unique experience for us

- Isaiah Lim for pulling the research information together

- My global coauthors who endured the Thursday evening calls (Friday morning in Sydney) for two and a half years, successfully and skillfully taking our manuscript all the way to publication

Robert A. Cooke

I gratefully acknowledge the contributions of:

- David Castro for everything he did to get the Quantum Edition of our Transglobal Leadership Survey online and tested for administration to our leaders

- Jessica Cooke and other members of the team at Human Synergistics for their invaluable contributions, including putting together the reports for our leaders to provide them with feedback on their survey responses

- Our global leaders not only for responding to our survey with care but also for nominating others to describe them

- My coauthors for demonstrating how members of a diverse team can maintain their differentiated perspectives while crafting a multifaceted, integrated, and unique contribution to leadership research and development

Peter A. Barge

- Isaiah Lim, my PA back in our Jones Lang LaSalle days, for his dedicated support and search wizardry

- Colin Dyer, my ex-boss, for giving his direct reports encouragement and space to pursue outside projects, board positions, and activities that made us more rounded and better leaders

- My fellow authors who all brought a unique set of skills, life experiences, and perspectives to the project

- The 150 leaders who took the time out of their busy schedule to complete the survey, many of whom made time to sit down and tell their story and reflect on their journey to becoming transglobal leaders

THE CURRENT STATE OF GLOBAL LEADERSHIP TALENT AND WHY GLOBAL LEADERS MATTER FOR BUSINESS SUCCESS

This part of the book will take you through the relevance and importance of effective global leadership. It will help you understand why this topic is so critically important in today's increasingly global world of work and why there's intense competition for successful global leaders. This is especially true for those leaders who can integrate effectively across countries, cultures, and geographies.

Chapter 1 frames the book and provides the context and background for our study. In this chapter, we discuss the concept of the book and what you will learn by reading it. You will also have the opportunity to take an abridged version of the Transglobal Leadership Survey (Table 1.1) to give you an indication of your personal capacity to lead in the global business world or to assess someone you are thinking about putting into a global role.

Chapter 2 will take you through many stories and experiences that illustrate what happens to a company's performance if it does not have the global talent to help the enterprise move forward. This chapter underscores the reasons why global talent is in such short supply and how the complexity of the global environment creates challenges that most companies are ill equipped to deal with.

Chapter 3 highlights the various forms of intelligence that were considered in constructing our survey and that global leaders need to be aware of to be successful. We describe five forms of intelligence in addition to the required cognitive intelligence necessary to function in the business world today. These other forms of intelligence are foundational and are emphasized to raise the awareness of leaders and to help them identify gaps that can be addressed.

Chapter 4 goes into the detail of our study and the underlying premise and assumptions that informed our research. Here we cover exactly how we conducted the research and what we learned. You will see the survey design and layout, and more importantly, you will see that this research is unique and different from other studies in that it compares the transglobal leadership dimensions to a robust Human Synergistics database on leaders.

CHAPTER 1

Survival in a New Global World: Are You Ready?

They are worth their weight in gold, and if you have them, you had better hold on to them because everyone else is short of them.

—Steve Bertamini, Group Executive Director and CEO of Standard Chartered Global Consumer Banking

Bertamini is talking about leaders who can shine in global roles can be difficult to find. If you play on the global stage, you will come across successful global leaders in a wide range of industries, in all parts of the world, and at all levels within the corporation. Those leaders who can "hit the ground running" when assigned to a new country or a different role are a rare but growing group. You can move them across geographies, across business lines, and even across companies. They have the personal and business stamina that enables them to lead and motivate diverse teams, balance the local and global needs of multinational corporations, and understand how business works. And they can do it in a way that delivers results while juggling complex and somewhat inconsistent ethical standards across countries.

Corporations are constantly scouting for successful leaders, especially those who can integrate effectively across countries, cultures, and geographies, and there is fierce competition for this global leader talent pool. "When we find them, we support them, value them, and try to clone them," said Clayton Daley, the recently retired vice chairman and CFO of Procter & Gamble.

After years of working with leaders in all parts of the world, studying leadership behavior, and coaching leaders, we have come to the conclusion that current constructs for leadership no longer work as well in the global arena as in the local arena. What is most startling is that as business becomes more global, poor leadership becomes more obvious more quickly, and it can be far more detrimental. The leaders who are placed in global assignments can either help the business "spiral up" and achieve great results or "spiral down" and achieve limited results or, in some cases, flat out fail!

We have watched many times as experienced leaders who have been put in expatriate assignments fail, but we have also seen some leaders navigate the new territory with elegance and ease. We asked ourselves why some leaders were so successful, and why some who were highly successful in their home countries were marginal at best or failed miserably when they were posted offshore. In our work, we have not attempted to map leadership DNA because it is a moving target, but what we have researched are the qualities and behaviors that are, in most cases, the minimum, nonnegotiable characteristics found in the hundreds of successful global leaders we have observed. As we traveled across multiple borders and collected hundreds of stories and anecdotes, we began to see common themes emerge. They formed the underpinnings of our theory, the study we decided to launch, and the basis for this book.

We observed companies that would select, for global assignments, successful or up-and-coming leaders from one environment or culture and watch as a small group of these selected leaders hit the ground running, while a larger number never lived up to the company's expectations. That led us to ask why. What did one group do that was different from the other?

We set out to discover if there were key factors that enabled some of these leaders to be so successful. We wanted to identify the following:

- What did they do specifically that made them so good?

- What were their unique characteristics that set them apart?

- How did they develop these characteristics?

If we could uncover the special aspects or dimensions that these great leaders embodied, we would have uncovered the "holy grail" for successful global leadership that could be replicated anywhere in the world. We believe that understanding this essence of global leadership will save organizations lots of time, spare them embarrassing mistakes, and ultimately save them money as they endeavor to build successful businesses off their home shores.

WHY THIS BOOK IS IMPORTANT

This book is particularly timely now, as hardly any organization can escape the impact of globalization—whether they are trying to do business in other parts of the world or they have suppliers and customers from outside their national borders. In the past, poor leadership outside of home markets could have been overlooked or gone unnoticed. In those early days, communication was not what it is today, and organizations were just beginning to learn what to do and how to operate outside their own cultures. Leadership mistakes were often overlooked or went unnoticed as companies tentatively felt their way forward. Expatriates and their families were widely supported financially. Often, they were insulated from the new country or they had slower-than-optimal transitions as a result of living in small enclaves of other expatriates, thus maintaining their sense of a "back-home" community.

In the early days of overseas expansion, the impact of errors in leadership was often not fully understood by the home country because of language barriers. Also, newly transferred managers seemed to have more time to settle in, allowing them to get their bearings, assimilate to their new surroundings, learn from their mistakes, and grow into the job. Local talent tolerated their mishaps. But with the fast pace of business and speed of technology today, this "settling-in time" is no longer possible. Mistakes are communicated with lightning speed around the globe, cutting leaders no slack.

Companies become global overnight, as did MetLife when it acquired Alico, formerly part of AIG. Whether they like it or not, they now have a global company with lots of leaders who have different beliefs, values, and, in some cases, dramatically divergent points of view. Joint ventures (JVs) are seen as ways to get quickly into new markets. Yesterday, a company may have had some multinational outposts, but after the JV, suddenly it has a broad footprint in many parts of the globe that it is unprepared for and unfamiliar with. A perfect example is the merger of Hewlett-Packard (HP) and Compaq, which put HP in many more countries than it had ever operated in before. HP did a great job of integrating the two companies; however, the integration challenges were enormous and widely publicized. The point is, hardly anyone can escape globalization today. Companies are outsourcing work off their shores, buying companies in far reaches of the globe, and creating strategic partnerships in places that they would not have thought of just 10 years ago.

Customers are also becoming increasingly global. They are demanding that their suppliers support them with top-quality services and products wherever they do business. Customers' needs for global services put pressure on any business that wants to succeed in this new world to become global overnight. Even if your operations are not particularly global today, tomorrow they will be—and must be—if you want to be competitive and service your global customers' needs.

Pandora's Box has been opened, and there is no going back to the way business was done in the past. Successful businesses that can compete in this "new normal" global world quickly realize that it is the talent, particularly the leadership talent, that is the critical variable in the formula for success. Businesses simply must have the talent to compete, and they can't wait for years to develop that talent—it will be too late. They must have the leaders who can build the company presence, attract and retain great talent in new markets, and build a sustainable company brand—or the game is over!

You might be saying at this point that needing great leaders is nothing new. We have always known that leadership is a critical differentiator between successful and unsuccessful companies. You are right: it always has been, but the global stage only heightens the need and puts a spotlight on poor leadership as never before. In the global arena the lack of leadership capability becomes magnified and much more visible. The real issue is that global leadership must deal with a staggering amount of complexity in a way that local leaders have never had to. It takes a special kind of leader to deal with the complex legal, cultural, political, and social environments that globalization presents.

We think of an often-used example that makes our point: Fred Astaire, the world-renowned dancer, could be akin to a wonderful local leader. He could dance any dance masterfully. But Ginger Rogers, his partner, could be compared to a great global leader. She danced masterfully but in much more complex circumstances (backward and in high heels). A great leader may be able to function well in his or her local markets, but without certain knowledge and behaviors, he or she will be marginalized in global markets. There are important differences between great local leaders and great global leaders, and this book clearly defines these differences. What really makes a global leader's job so hard is exemplified in the following quote from Ranjay Gulati, The Jaime and Josefina Chua Tiampo Professor of Business Administration, Harvard Business School:

> Many global situations are not only complex but also ambiguous. The global world also creates a high degree of uncertainty. It's the combination of the ambiguity, complexity, and uncertainty that makes the global leader's job so very difficult.

FOUR CLASSIC LEADERSHIP SYNDROMES

We have seen four classic syndromes play out over and over in our own travels around the world where ill-prepared leaders have created problems and gotten themselves derailed, and in some cases they were not able to recover. They are:

- **The egocentric syndrome.** "Things can be done only the way the home country does them. It's our way or the highway!"

- **The language syndrome.** "The best leaders speak my language. If I can understand them, they must be good."

- **The Western syndrome.** "We're from the West, and we have been building and developing businesses longer than you, so we are smarter at it."

- **The cultural assumption syndrome.** "We assume we know the other party's culture and that what is relevant in our culture is relevant elsewhere."

The impacts of these syndromes can be devastating if organizations don't focus on developing the leadership talent that can compete globally. Here are true stories from our collective experiences that painfully demonstrate how each syndrome manifests itself in poor overseas leadership.

The Egocentric Syndrome

A very senior American banker was assigned to run an operation in London to cover the whole of Europe's foreign exchange for the bank. She had her first meeting with her new team—over 400 people. She started the meeting by introducing herself and reinforcing that she was now in charge. She then proceeded to inform the group that she did not care how things were done in London or in Europe for that matter. Instead, things would have to be done as they were in the United States. Her egocentric approach caused everyone in the room to flinch. You could visibly see the eyes roll in the room, but the leader was oblivious to her impact. Obviously, banking in the United Kingdom and the rest of Europe could not be done as it was being done in the United States. Clearly the complexity in Europe was too vast across the geography, a fact that this leader completely failed to appreciate.

The Language Syndrome

Another example we witnessed was that of a new leader who had been sent to Japan in the mid-1990s during the Japanese economic and technological frenzy. This leader gravitated to those Japanese who spoke good English, usually younger talent who had some overseas experience as opposed to those who were really respected by the Japanese team members and could make things happen (or more important, not happen). The Western leader took for granted that the English-speaking talent must be good because they spoke his language.

But he was clearly wrong. As a result, the expatriate leader could not gain the respect of the Japanese staff, and he was instead surrounded by less competent players. He promoted the good English speakers, and ultimately, the venture lost money because it could not gain traction in the local market. The newly promoted Japanese leaders in charge did not have the credibility, experience, or maturity in the eyes of other employees that were necessary for the business to succeed.

As Richard Solomons, chief executive officer, InterContinental Hotels Group (IHG), sees it, "It is a big mistake to assume that if someone speaks your language you have a common understanding of each other's culture—wrong!"

THE WESTERN SYNDROME

In a similar case, a leader was trying to establish a joint venture in another Asian territory. He completely disregarded local customs and culture, talked down to the potential partners, disregarded their suggestions, and generally behaved like the proverbial "bull in a china shop." Needless to say, the negotiations broke down, and the joint venture never went through, at great cost.

THE CULTURAL ASSUMPTION SYNDROME

A perfect example of this final syndrome comes from India, a country to which many businesses have moved or expanded. This particular leader believed that he understood how the local team thought. He would meet with the team, and they would appear to nod in agreement on a plan. As he waited for the plans to materialize, however, he saw no progress. He was later informed that nodding in India, and a number of other countries, does not necessarily imply agreement.

David Jacobs, former chairman Asia Pacific of the global law firm Baker & McKenzie, recounted the personal experience he had with this syndrome: "I was at a partners' retreat at one of my Asian offices. I noted a number of partners kept walking in and out, were talking on their cells and texting. I was getting annoyed and thought it was rude and discourteous. During my presentation, I noted this conduct and suggested it was disrespectful to their colleagues. I suspect my Asian partners were offended by my comments, as I subsequently learned this was acceptable conduct in their culture. In retrospect, I should have checked in with them to understand how they were reacting to see if it was an issue. This was a classic example of me imposing my culture on them, and it was wrong."

These stories are just a few of the many that we have witnessed over the years. The syndromes they describe have repeated themselves time and time again and have gotten in the way of business success. As the world becomes increasingly more global, these missteps become ever more evident and more widely communicated. This quote from Richard Solomons, CEO of IHG, sums things up well: "Wherever you are assigned or whatever new role or environment you find yourself in, your first priority is to be inquisitive to succeed. It is simply no good going into a new role thinking you know how the world works and you don't."

We have also seen countless examples of companies that have succeeded in the global environment and continue to do so today. They have developed outstanding leaders who can function anywhere in the world. We are not saying that these companies did not have some bumps in the road in developing global leaders and opening new markets. They certainly did. However, they seem to be able to learn from their mistakes, they continue to perfect their approaches, and they are generally considered successful today. We will discuss some of these exemplars in depth, such as Procter & Gamble, Disney, McDonald's, HP, GE, Standard Chartered Bank, IHG, and Jones Lang LaSalle, to name a few. We think this point from Richard Solomons sums up the leadership attitudes of these successful companies: "One reason IHG has been more successful than its traditional competitors is that we never think or talk about being 'international.' We talk about being 'global.' A number of our larger competitors are divided geographically as U.S. and international divisions. This sends the wrong message. Other hotel chains have not been as successful as IHG around the world because they act overseas just as they act in their home country."

THE INTERCONNECTIVITY OF
THE NEW BUSINESS WORLD

In this increasingly global business environment, economies, businesses, and governments are powerfully interconnected. Having globally savvy leaders is essential; it is not merely a "nice to have." What happens in one part of the globe can have significant effects on the other parts. Let's reflect back on September 11, 2001. This tragedy and its aftermath revealed how interconnected the world is. We are not sure anyone really understood the degree of this interconnectedness until then, when a single series of events in the United States had repercussions around the world. Commerce as we knew it literally stopped. People all over the world were stranded. For months afterward, hotels were virtually empty and big corporate events were canceled. The impact was enormous, very visible, and painful. New processes and procedures (like airport security checks) were instituted everywhere in the world and may never go away.

Fast forward and we again see the interconnectedness. The economic meltdown that started in the United States in 2008 has impacted just about every part of the global economy. Very little of the rest of the world has escaped the impact of that meltdown. In a trip to China, we observed that several manufacturing plants were laying off workers because demand for goods and services in the mature markets had dwindled due to consumption retrenchment. The eurozone economic crisis had the world jittery, and the 2011 tsunami in Japan severely impacted the ability of global companies to secure parts and deliver equipment needed for the assembly of products in other parts of the world. Every country in the world that employs nuclear power watched closely to see how the Japanese nuclear plants were being stabilized.

We cannot escape how we are now entwined, and by all predictions, the interdependencies will increase at an even faster pace. Couple this interconnectedness with the speed of technology, and the impact on businesses and leaders is dizzying. As time goes on, we will be ever more embedded in each other's economies. Having leaders who can be flexible and can synchronize with the emerging and ever-more-global nature of the business world is tantamount. It is the leadership and the people that will separate the victorious from those who merely survive, or worse, perish in the "perfect storm." It is the leadership talent that will make or break a company as it moves more and more into the global arena, either by accident or by strategic and deliberate choice.

At the 2011 World Economic Forum in Davos, Switzerland, one of the top issues that concerned the CEOs who attended was their ability to attract and retain talent that could function successfully in new and emerging global markets. In their yearly report of CEO concerns, PricewaterhouseCoopers (PwC) underscored this point as front and center in the minds of CEOs today. Having missteps in leadership can no longer be tolerated. The plain fact is that you can have all the technology in the world, great cash reserves, and good business fundamentals, but in the global arena, the real key to success is the people. Without great global leaders, you run a sizable risk of losing momentum in what will continue to be the ever-expanding world arena.

WHY YOU SHOULD READ THIS BOOK

We set out to understand the fundamental differences between good leaders and outstanding global leaders and, more importantly, how to find and develop them. Through this effort, we uncovered the critical behavioral dimensions that separate these great global leaders from others. You will be surprised to see how clear these dimensions are. When you read this book you will learn the following:

- The critical foundation of global leadership intelligence

- The five behavioral dimensions relevant to identifying successful global leaders

- How to understand the difference between the characteristics of global leaders and those of leaders who function more effectively in their home environments

- How to identify great global leaders using our Transglobal Leadership Matrix

- How to assess your organization for its ability to compete on a global scale

- The keys to assessing talent for global capability early in careers

- What to do to develop, nurture, and retain high-performing global talent

- What diversity looks like in the new world order

This is a practical book based on the real-life experiences of the authors, who have each worked in or consulted with large global companies all over the world for more than 20 years. But what really sets this book apart is that its findings and recommendations are supported by research, analysis, and statistical evidence. Unlike some other leadership books out there, we have not written a book based only on theory, observation, and opinions. Instead, we provide hard evidence based on survey research into what leaders need to do to drive results globally. We know from both a qualitative and quantitative perspective that our five behavioral dimensions provide the formula for creating high-performing global leaders and therefore, high-performance organization cultures. If your company wants to succeed in the global market, you must have leaders who put these behaviors into practice.

WHAT WE DID

We constructed a survey based on the literature, refined it many times, and examined more than 150 successful global leaders in companies such as Baker & McKenzie, IHG, Jones Lang LaSalle, Hewlett-Packard, General Electric, Standard Chartered Bank, Accenture, Microsoft, Accor, and Unilever. We looked for successful leaders who came from diverse companies of various sizes across industry types, from multiple geographical headquarters. We identified and surveyed individuals who had successfully transcended economic and business turbulence and who had effectively traversed various cultures and geographies.

We then analyzed the survey results and followed up with extensive interviews to understand specifically what these leaders did that made them so successful. Then we compared them to the leaders in the Human Synergistics database of over 5,000 leaders, an extensive compilation of leaders who, in the main, operated in their home country. Human Synergistics has well over 1 million data samples on leaders and managers, but this database was picked primarily because it was global in nature and included senior organization leaders. We surveyed peers and colleagues of our leadership sample to determine their impact on others and how they created constructive organization cultures that delivered effective business results. What we discovered are the five behavioral dimensions of successful global leaders. These five behavioral dimensions, we believe, are the key to your leadership and business success. We call it *transglobal leadership*.

THE THREE PARTS OF THE BOOK

Part I provides the background for the research, describes its design and analysis, and summarizes how we conducted our study. We define the underpinnings and foundation of global leadership as possessing the necessary intelligence for global assignments, the intelligence that is tantamount for a leader to have to function effectively on a global scale. This intelligence is composed of six areas, based on the literature, that characterize successful global leaders:

Cognitive. Their intellectual horsepower

Moral. Their ethical compass

Emotional. Their ability to relate to and empathize with others

Cultural. Their ability to adapt effectively to various cultural contexts

Business. Their understanding of how business functions and the interconnectedness of the respective parts of an organization

Global. Their ability to execute their jobs in a global context and balance global standardization with local flexibility

In this part, we define and describe these elements of intelligence and explain what successful leaders need to know about each. We outline a prescription for success and present a model that will ensure the development of highly successful global leaders who can achieve high-performing cultures and businesses.

Part II identifies and explains the five behavioral dimensions of transglobal leaders and presents the Transglobal Leadership Matrix. The dimensions are these:

Uncertainty resilience. Building on differences and complexity. The ability of leaders to deal with ambiguity, complexity, and differences. These transglobal leaders can effectively function in highly unclear situations and do not become paralyzed by them.

Team connectivity. Integrating across boundaries. These transglobal leaders focus on the success of the teams in organizations, and they work across boundaries, supported by traditional notions of organizational teams.

Pragmatic flexibility. Adapting to other cultures. These transglobal leaders will carefully adjust their values to get the job done. They emphasize the needs of the work group rather than their own. They are highly adaptive to others' cultures.

Perceptive responsiveness. Acting on intuition and fact. These transglobal leaders see the differences between people and anticipate the changing needs of customers and other key stakeholders. They are highly sensitive to others' needs and reactions.

Talent orientation. Achieving through people. These transglobal leaders are personally engaged in talent development, and they do not rely exclusively on others (i.e., HR departments) to develop their people.

The Transglobal Leadership Matrix defines and describes leaders by each dimension and explains how they think, make decisions, communicate, build teams, and are viewed by others.

Most importantly, Part II highlights what these leaders do to build sustainable businesses anywhere. Examples, stories, and case studies are provided to shed light on the specific approaches they use. A focal point of this discussion is demonstrating how these individuals approach diversity. Clearly, a new order is emerging that we believe will change the way companies and global organizations address diversity and inclusion. We share what they do to take traditional diversity issues to the next level and create truly global inclusive teams. These leaders are the beacons of a new global order of diversity for their organizations.

Part III provides tools, techniques, and tips to assist you in assessing your organization, teams, and leaders for their global leadership acumen. The identification of talent for global capability early in people's careers will enable you to build a future pipeline of talent. We give you a lens through which to spot and recruit potential global talent. Perhaps most importantly are the specific methods and best practices we provide for developing, nurturing, and retaining global talent once you find them.

The book ends as it begins with a methodology outlining how to assess yourself for your own global leadership capability, along with suggestions for what you can do to increase your organization's, team's, and personal global leadership effectiveness.

WHO SHOULD READ THIS BOOK?

This book is a call to action for anyone in the global marketplace. It is a book designed for anyone looking to be successful in the global business environment today and tomorrow. It is an essential read whether you are a CEO of a company looking to expand to emerging markets, or a manager or leader looking to develop your personal capability in leading in the global arena, or a board member trying to navigate through global waters with a solid company strategy. If you are a human resources leader or responsible for organization development or leadership development for your company, this is a practical guide for what you can do to assess and build global talent.

If you are just starting your career and want to expand globally, this book will help you identify what you need to do to enhance your global skills. Don't think that if you aren't yet in a global role or assignment that this book does not pertain to you. It does! This book will provide you with invaluable insights for dealing with the increasingly diverse global talent that is in your workplace today and will be there in increasing numbers in the immediate years to come. Global talent is at your doorstep, and the question is: Are you ready to embrace it? In a nutshell, this book is a critical read for any leader or manager or person doing business today.

Now if you still are not compelled to take the deep plunge into this book, we suggest that you reflect on and ask yourself the questions that follow. If you can't answer them or they give you heartburn when you think about the possible answers, you must read this book!

Questions

For the Board of Directors

- Look around the boardroom: how truly diverse are the board members?

- How well would the CEO and the senior management team perform if they responded honestly to the personal statements in Table 1.1?

- How deep and global is the succession plan for the senior management team?

- Where are the real decisions made in this organization: is there a headquarters culture?

- Does the board have exposure to a broad cross-section of the business and its customers, and do meetings rotate around the business?

- How open, inclusive, and welcoming is the culture to outsiders, new ideas, and alternative ways of looking at and doing things?

For the Senior Management Team

- Look around the team: how truly diverse is it? Does it reflect the geography and current and emerging nature of the business?

- Are your succession candidates diverse or do they mirror the incumbent?

- Do you personally support, both financially and intellectually, a culture of global development and mobility?

- When you need to cut costs, where have training and mobility typically been on that list?

- If you analyzed your calendar for the last month, would you have spent more than 30 percent of your time directly involved in people and talent matters?

- Do you give the field "freedom within a framework," or is it very much a head office culture when it comes to important decisions?

- How successful have your leaders been in expat assignments, and how has this been measured?

For Human Resources Leadership

- Are your expats primarily from the headquarters' country, or are they also selected from elsewhere?

- Do you scramble to find expat candidates for global assignments?

- Do you have difficulties with repatriation?

- Are assignments made just to fill a seat, or are they thoughtful and strategic development moves?

- Do you have talent management tools for global talent and succession, and do you differentiate those tools with respect to global versus local assignments?

- Do you rigorously assess your leaders' capabilities for global assignments?

- How global is your succession management process?

CONCLUSION

Before you dig deeper into this book, respond to the 10 sets of opposing statements in Table 1.1 either in terms of your own thinking and behavioral styles or those of a current or potential global leader in your organization. These 10 sets are 10 of the 71 sets in the full, original Transglobal Leadership Survey. If you're describing yourself, this is your personal call to action to get prepared to compete in the brave new world of globalization.

When you select a response between each set of statements, please describe yourself as honestly as possible, and try to resist the temptation to provide the "right" answers. As hard as we tried to avoid doing so, many of our statements are nevertheless transparent, and the global answer can be readily discerned. However, if you focus on describing yourself the way others would describe you, rather than forcing the answers, the results will be of greater value to you. If you are a CEO, an HR executive, or another leader responsible for filling global positions, you can instead describe one of your global leaders or another person who is being considered for a key international position.

The statements in each pair in Table 1.1 represent alternatives that might be descriptive of you. Compare the two alternatives, and decide which one more accurately describes your behavior as a manager. Then, select one of the seven response options given.

Table 1.1 Transglobal Leadership Survey Descriptive Statements

	1	2	3	4	5	6	7	
Seek out projects and assignments that are new and different.	1	2	3	4	5	6	7	Seek out projects and assignments that are familiar and comfortable.
Respond to diverse and subtle expressions of disagreement.	1	2	3	4	5	6	7	Assume agreement unless others differ in a direct and overt manner.
Stay detached and focus on accomplishing the task.	1	2	3	4	5	6	7	Show compassion even if it jeopardizes the task at hand.
Adjust own activities to enhance the performance of others.	1	2	3	4	5	6	7	Design own activities to maximize personal performance.
Emphasize rules, formal procedures, and how things are supposed to work.	1	2	3	4	5	6	7	Emphasize norms, the informal network, and how things really get done.
Take budgets seriously and live within the constraints they impose.	1	2	3	4	5	6	7	Work with and adjust budgets in response to current business dynamics.
Assume that local concerns and values can adjust to corporate policies.	1	2	3	4	5	6	7	Assume that corporate policies can adjust to local (country-specific) concerns.
Anticipate the changing needs of customers.	1	2	3	4	5	6	7	Identify customers' needs on the basis of their current buying habits.
Provide others with specific feedback on their performance on a regular basis.	1	2	3	4	5	6	7	Provide others with feedback infrequently or only during formal reviews.
Use people and human resource development as strategic levers.	1	2	3	4	5	6	7	Use technology and process as strategic levers.

Source: Adapted from Robert A. Cooke, Peter A. Barge, Nazneen Razi, and Linda D. Sharkey, the Transglobal Leadership Survey—Quantum Edition with permission. Copyright 2010 by Human Synergistics International. All rights reserved.

If the left statement more accurately describes you, circle one of the three options to the left of the middle number (4) using the guidelines below:

- 1 is almost exactly like the left statement.

- 2 is much like the left statement.

- 3 is somewhat like the left statement.

If the statement on the right is more accurate, select one of the three options to the right of the 4 using the guidelines below:

- 5 is somewhat like the right statement.

- 6 is much like the right statement.

- 7 is almost exactly like the right statement.

If neither alternative is more descriptive of you, select the middle option 4, which would be about equally like the left and right statements.

In Chapter 9, which is the last chapter, you can see how your responses compare with those of the global leaders we surveyed. You also can review your responses and see if your thoughts about any of them have changed after reading the book. We hope you enjoy the read.

CHAPTER 2

Why Global Talent Is So Important, Yet in Short Supply

Global leadership is so critically important. We cannot possibly compete effectively without it. However, today we can't get enough good leaders who can function in complex, multicultural environments to get done what needs to get done. Just because individuals have had a global assignment does not mean they are global leaders. Global leaders have the special ability to make things simple and understandable for others and connect to people in subtle but very powerful ways.

—Mark Hutchinson, CEO of GE China

The quote above from Mark Hutchinson, CEO of GE China, highlights the talent problems that face everyone. He clearly understands that the key to success is the talent he can assemble in China. He knows this talent is what he needs to move the ball. This could be said by many leading CEOs.

Yet why is it that scientists have successfully mapped the human genome, but after the thousands of books and research studies on leadership, the goalposts of success seem to be continually moving and changing? One reason is that unlike human DNA, which has needed to change very little in thousands of years, the leadership characteristics we need today are evolving at a pace commensurate with the velocity of business growth and change.

For many corporations, the requirement for successful leadership is not a mystery or a puzzle to be solved; rather, it is a journey to be followed. As a result of the speed of business, globalization, erosion of trust, war for talent, and the complexities of everyday life, the traits that successful leaders need to have, particularly successful global leaders, are continually evolving in tandem with their environment. What happens on the global leadership playing field epitomizes, more than ever, Charles Darwin's views (borrowing from Herbert Spencer) on "the survival of the fittest": the most adaptable leaders who persevere will be the leaders who succeed in the ever-changing global business environment.

THE COMPLEXITY OF THE GLOBAL ENVIRONMENT

Years of working with and developing leaders in global companies using existing leadership models and assessment tools has often resulted in unacceptably low success rates when those leaders were asked to operate outside of the country where their experience and knowledge had been acquired. Existing leadership constructs seem inadequate and inconsistent in the context of the new challenges that continue to face companies as they become increasingly more global.

It has become obvious to us that the world is more demanding and less forgiving of a leader's mistakes today than ever before. As a result of the growing array of diverse cultures combined with the complexities of global business, ill-equipped and ill-prepared leaders find a minefield awaiting them when they are posted offshore. HR practitioners will confirm that finding a successful leader has been a hit-or-miss exercise. The hits tend to have a lot to do with the expatriate leader having time to work through the cultural and global challenges and settle in. Unfortunately, leaders are rarely afforded the luxury of time. The connected world and the emergence of social networks and communication forums, such as Facebook, LinkedIn, Twitter, and blogs have made the role and effectiveness of the newly arrived leader highly transparent and continually scrutinized.

Let's look at this example. A CEO who was being transferred from his home country to a new region made a couple of negative comments about the organizational structure in the country where he was to be posted. Even before he arrived at his new location, the chat rooms were replete with speculations on the changes that he would make. His new team had already formed a very negative opinion based on the web "buzz" that had spread like wildfire.

Effective communication has always been an important leadership characteristic. In today's world of rapid and instant communication, however, a leader has to be acutely sensitive to the environment and to ever-increasing and expanding communication channels. Leaders today must move with a greater degree of urgency than was expected in prior times. In new and unfamiliar surroundings, this is very difficult for many.

Ranjay Gulati puts it this way: "A lot of expats implode from day one, particularly the confident and successful ones, in their home market. They cannot see their own implosions, and they are often difficult to coach because in their mind it is rarely their fault, and they start to blame everything and everyone else. You'll often hear them say, 'Locals are losers. I need to clean house anyway, and

I need a new team to get things done.' These people are just not clued in. They lack cultural sensibilities—the basic requirements. If you see silence as incompetence in the West and think that is what it means elsewhere, you're in big trouble, as in the Asian context, silence may mean deference."

Leaders, particularly CEOs, are under increasing pressure. The demands for growth, the increase in intensity of competition, and the challenges of globalization can test even the most experienced leader. Nothing has added more complexity to the leadership equation than globalization. Joint ventures and acquisitions are becoming a way of life for companies to continue to grow in new markets. As leaders move around geographically, the challenges are daunting. The two big homes of multinationals—the United States and Europe—are running out of steam in many of their home markets, and more enticing growth opportunities offered by other emerging markets are looming even larger. According to Clayton Daley, retired vice chairman and CFO of Procter & Gamble, the "skill set of the people and leaders you send in to integrate a global acquisition is critical. It's the know-it-alls, who tell everyone what to do and are not flexible and collaborative, that bring you down."

Finding talent to fuel and sustain this expansion and tap this growth potential is getting even tougher. While it has never been easy, it's much more daunting now. A study of expatriates in over 750 U.S., European, and Japanese companies found that 10 to 20 percent of American managers sent abroad returned early because of job dissatisfaction or difficulties personally or with family members in adjusting to a foreign country.[1] Of those who stayed for the entire duration, nearly 33 percent did not perform up to the expectations of their superiors. A full 25 percent who did complete their assignment left their company to join a competitor within one year after repatriation. The turnover rate of this group was double that of managers who did not go abroad.

The costs of this turnover and mis-hires are astronomical. Gary Budzinski, former senior vice president for Hewlett-

Packard's technical services division, who led a global team of over 40,000 employees in 170 countries, sums it up much the way Mark Hutchinson at GE does. According to Budzinski: "Just because people have worked globally, it doesn't mean they have a global mindset. And just because people haven't worked globally, it doesn't mean they can't function well in a global environment. What makes for the global mindset is being extremely self-aware and being willing to develop the personal skills and behaviors to make something meaningful out of the global experiences and to learn. Being willing to learn is essential."

Finding this talent and keeping it are what make or break a company in terms of success. If you are not careful about whom you select and you don't select the right leaders, you run a great risk of people and the organization derailing. According to Quint Studer, author of *Hardwiring Excellence*, 39 percent of the employees who leave an organization leave because of their boss. While the mishire of the leader can be costly and tragic, the greater impact on the larger workforce can be even more costly! We won't even begin to talk about the impact on customer relations when a company's turnover is high.

WHY ARE THESE LEADERS IN SUCH SHORT SUPPLY?

The simple reason is that there are too many leadership competency models that are not well adapted to the global leadership arena; none that we know of has been proven to yield real, positive results. There is a dire need for a crisp and simple model that focuses on critical global elements. To paraphrase what Sandy Ogg, former chief human resources officer (CHRO) for Unilever and now CHRO for Blackstone, said at a 2008 Conference at INSEAD: There are way too many competencies out there describing leadership. No one can possess all of these competencies. What we need is a simple construct that makes sense for what is important for global leadership.

Companies come up with complicated and untested leadership constructs that they use when the global talent issue is at their door. Instead, they should plan for the inevitability that they will need talent that can function anywhere in the world. In our own experience, we have seen the following:

- Companies have not focused on developing global leaders. Most companies have leadership programs of some sort, but the emphasis is not on the global nature of work. Many of these leadership programs or initiatives are provided later in the career when much of how a leader functions and behaves has already been formed. In many cases, leaders have to unlearn behaviors, stop doing things that made them successful in the past, or relearn skills. We have not seen methods for early testing of global acumen and development of talent that can ultimately take on bigger, broader, and more globally complex assignments. There are some companies that focus on early global talent pipeline development, like Procter & Gamble, GE, and McDonald's, but this certainly is not the norm.

- Even if they've recognized the need to do so, many companies haven't known how to develop global leaders. It has often been assumed that if you put leaders on global assignment with some cultural and language training, they can figure out how to lead anywhere if they are smart. Or leaders have routinely been put through a long list of competency-based training activities, none of which has been validated to make a difference in their ability to lead in a global environment. The assumption is made that if leaders are good at leading, they can lead anywhere. Maybe they can, and maybe they can't, but making this assumption can be very costly.

- By the time leaders get to a global assignment or have to lead a global team, many leaders see the world from where they hail. The danger of seeing issues and processes from one's own context is that processes and leadership styles that work in India will not necessarily work in Australia. The pitfalls of transporting business approaches from one geography to another can be numerous: one size does not fit all. McDonald's, one of the pioneers in the global leadership context, learned this lesson early on. A McDonald's in Paris cannot look like a McDonald's in the United States, nor serve the same basic burger. Starbucks initially decided not to compete in Italy, where coffee is an art form, before reconsidering.

- According to David Qu, general manager for Fiberweb China and also a former director for Procter & Gamble (P&G), after some missteps of trying to move a consistent compliance process around the world, P&G learned that these processes had to be adapted and adjusted for the local market so that people could understand and apply them in their own context. Senior P&G leaders thought that the local country managers were resistant to change, but in actuality, they did not understand how the processes and programs fit into their local environment. Once they did understand and put the change in their own context, it was smooth sailing.

- The types of intelligence needed for global success are neither well articulated nor adequately understood. Much has been written about cognitive intelligence, as measured by the intelligence quotient (IQ), as the foundation for leadership. Though we agree with this, a high IQ will not by itself make a global leader. Malcolm Gladwell in *Outliers* studied many people with above average or outstanding IQs.[2] He found that it was a variety of characteristics that made some people more successful than others. Some of the people he studied were not successful at all even though they possessed superior IQs. Sadly, even with all that has been written about leadership and all the training that goes on in companies relative to developing leaders, leaders are still promoted based on their technical skills and ability to execute. Many organizations don't understand the multifaceted requirements for global leadership intelligence.

- There is a real lack of understanding of what the behavioral requirements are for truly global leaders. Many companies assume they know the behaviors required, but very few have studied their really successful global leaders to understand what they do differently as compared to those who are not as successful. These companies use something like the leadership "sheep dip" approach outlined in the second point above: they provide training in a long list of competencies. Companies have not defined what great global leadership looks like in clear and simple terms. They have not created the "best-in-class profile" for global leaders that provides the benchmark for success. Most companies may have only a limited understanding of the subtle behaviors required for success, let alone know how to articulate them and measure them so that leaders understand what will help them or derail them as they go offshore.

Finding talent that can be successful in any geography has never been easy, but today this talent is a critical part of the growth equation for any company looking to expand beyond its own borders.

THE BUSINESS CONSEQUENCES OF
NOT HAVING EFFECTIVE GLOBAL LEADERS

Leaders' missteps can have serious repercussions from which recovery can take years, if recovery is even possible. As this chapter's opening quote by Mark Hutchinson (CEO of GE China) describes, the war for talent continues to be waged, particularly for high-value talent. He goes on to say: "It is the team that surrounds you that makes the real difference. Finding the right players that you can trust to build the relationships necessary to function successfully is really a new global leader's first job." There is also a need to be a great leader to attract this talent. Hutchinson says: "I must be humble, respectful, and really listen for meaning to be known as a leader people want to work for."

There is a significant premium being paid for high-performing global leaders. Research continues to show that people leave bosses, not necessarily companies, and although an economic downturn may slow down some of the churn, it does not keep a dissatisfied key performer from leaving to work for better leadership and better opportunity. Even companies that are downsizing are capitalizing on the current situation to upgrade their workforce, address marginal performers, and find ways to retain top talent. Many global companies entice high-performing talent through the promise of career growth and a strong leadership brand, but more and more, talented people are looking to the leader they will work under as a key determinant of whether they will move. Turnover rates are notoriously high in emerging markets. Employees in companies doing business in such markets have lots of options once minimum levels of experience are achieved. These employees know that they don't have to stay with a boss or company they don't like, for there is someone down the road who is just as happy to hire them. Lack of good global leadership will only exacerbate this continuing attrition.

Another serious repercussion is the impact on the brand and the unintended consequences of having poor leadership decision making or relationships with local government leaders. Leaders have come into new markets and not been able to work effectively with influential local leaders. Steven Levy highlights these issues relative to Google's foray into China in his book *In the Plex: How Google Thinks, Works, and Shapes Our Lives.* He cites that Google was imposing an American-centric point of view about how the Internet should work, which is not how China operates relative to freedom of information. It has been widely reported in the press that Google is at odds with the Chinese government. China is supporting a big competitor of Google's, Baidu. Google has been forced to retrench and adjust its approaches to gain respect and brand acceptance. Levy posits that the Google leaders needed coaching on how to behave in China and in India for that matter.[3] Having to retreat in a market with the potential of 1 billion users is significant, and having a formidable competitor emerge is also significant to Google's bottom- and top-line growth. We recognize that there may be disagreement about whether Google's approach was right and whether it was important to maintain free speech. Google's recent approach in Japan in providing assistance through Google Maps for the rebuilding effort after the tsunami has been reported in the press to be building trust and respect for the company—enabling Google to build the needed government relationship for continued expansion in Japan.

Another company embarked on a joint venture with a Chinese national manufacturing company. The leadership of the nonlocal partner was perceived by the Chinese leaders as not treating them respectfully. The Chinese leaders resisted any of the changes the leaders suggested, and an employee strike ensued. Of course, the nonlocal partner could not speak Chinese and did not know what messages were being transmitted to the employees. Obviously, though, the messages were not good, judging by the reaction and the level of hostility from the Chinese. The situation became so bad that there were death threats, and the entire joint venture fell apart. The plant was ultimately closed, costing losses in production and layoff fees, which added up to a tremendous sum of money for a company that did not have deep pockets. This is a great example of a company unnecessarily spiraling down into nonexistence in a market ripe for this company's product.

Even the U.S. military has admitted in news reports that it initially had arrogant approaches in dealing with the Iraqi military leaders. The military leaders learned the hard way that they had to change their tactics and gain a better understanding of the Iraqi military in order to move the war to the next phase of completion. The press has cited that lack of global leadership and misunderstanding of the Iraqi context may have cost more lives and prolonged the war unnecessarily.

Disney, which now enjoys huge global success, also had some hard lessons to learn at first. When the company built Disneyland Paris in 1992, it almost went bankrupt because of the way it was conceived in France. While Mickey Mouse is a universal figure, it was insufficient in attracting the French public. In addition, Disney failed to adopt a European, let alone French, flair. At least one glaring error was that wine was not permitted in the park's general kiosks. The corporate leadership clearly imposed a U.S.-based value that did not sit well with the French. Disney learned from these mistakes, and it has opened many successful global parks since. The newest park, scheduled to open in Shanghai in 2016, has been designed with the Chinese market in mind. It is uniquely Chinese in its layout, presentation, and architectural design. By all accounts, it is being applauded as a park cleverly and completely adapted to the local culture. It is expected to be a huge success.

There are many other examples, but we think you get the point. Failing to focus on building successful global leaders who will be your eyes and ears in new markets will ultimately and negatively impact your bottom line and business success. We have made the case for the cost impacts of turnover not only in staff members who leave a bad boss but also in failed leadership assignments. Sending the wrong people on expatriate assignments is extremely costly. Having to bring them home early due to poor performance is even more costly. The case has also been made that poor leadership in the market can impact your company's reputation, potential to get new business, and ability to retain quality staff. In some cases, it can impact your ability to get business done at all. We believe there is a new model of leadership that builds on the constructs of the *transformational leader*.

We are calling these leaders the *transglobal leaders*. These are the leaders who can play on the global stage with ease and grace. These are the leaders who are citizens of the world and who focus on building healthy and sustainable organizations wherever they are and regardless of who is making up the employee population. The remainder of the book will focus on these transglobal leaders: who they are and how you develop them for long-term innovation and growth.

SETTING THE STAGE FOR THE TRANSGLOBAL LEADER

We noted earlier that intelligence is the foundation for any effective leader; no one will dispute that fact. However, in the global context, intelligence takes on new meanings. It is not enough for leaders to have high cognitive intelligence, commonly referred to as IQ. The literature indicates that they must have other types of intelligence, which can be even more significant. These include the following:

Moral intelligence. Having a clear ethical compass and understanding how it plays out in different parts of the world.

Emotional intelligence. Empathizing and connecting with others on a social and emotional level. Being acutely aware of and intelligent about one's emotional capabilities is essential.

Cultural intelligence. Knowing the critical cultural norms and mores of the countries and areas in which one is assigned as a leader is tantamount to successful leadership. Leaders with this intelligence carefully learn and practice the cultural requirements necessary for success.

Business intelligence. Understanding the components of any successful business. Leaders with this form of intelligence operate from a framework that encompasses all the respective requirements from functional, process, data and information, and results points of view, not just from the financial perspective.

Global intelligence. Understanding the legal, economic, governmental, and procedural environment in which you will be functioning as a leader. Successful leaders with this intelligence learn how things are done in other parts of the world and do not assume that their own country's methods can be transported everywhere. They balance global standardization with local needs.

Taking the general cognitive intelligence as the initial entry point, leaders also need to possess the moral, emotional, cultural, global, and business intelligences to excel on a global level. While we do not believe that leaders can possess high levels of intelligence in all of these areas, we do insist that they need to be acutely aware of them in the global context, and they must have at least acceptable minimum levels of understanding across all of the above intelligences. Individuals will vary in their levels of strengths and weaknesses, but they must be able, at a minimum, to ask questions relative to these intelligence areas and get people around them who understand these areas in the country or geography in which they are working. Mark Hutchinson has expressed this point well. He cannot possibly be an expert in all the governmental relations and issues in China, but he has an "outstanding person" on his team "who is a real pro at building strong relationships. I just get out of his way and let him do his thing, and he does it well!" The transglobal leaders' colleagues become the support mechanism that will help fill gaps and remove blind spots, particularly in those critical early days of a new assignment.

CONCLUSION

Our point of departure is that successful transglobal leaders at a minimum are continually gaining and refining skills within and across multiple areas or intelligence, simultaneously. It is the mastery of skills within each of these intelligence areas that ultimately underpins their success, and they don't let their own ego get in the way when other people do a better job in some of these areas than they do. They celebrate their colleagues' success and get out of the way so their colleagues can do the job.

The literature suggests that each form of intelligence can be independently measured and tested, which is helpful because weakness in any one area can potentially limit the success of transglobal leaders.

What are the characteristics that can facilitate understanding, drive strategy, and deliver growth and results in the face of the ever-changing sets of new challenges presented to multinational corporations every day? By dissecting and measuring these facets of intelligence and by analyzing the data to understand them better, we were able to segregate the behavioral dimensions that are most essential for success. Individuals may not embody all the facets of intelligence we believe are necessary, but they must have the essential behavioral dimensions that we will discuss in detail in Part II. The foundational intelligence from which these behaviors were derived, however, cannot be ignored. These forms of intelligence and their relevance to selecting and developing successful transglobal leaders are defined in the next chapter.

The Foundation of the Transglobal Leader: The Six Facets of Intelligence Necessary for Transglobal Leadership

Before going to any international market or client, I make it a point to understand the current environment, the safety and political concerns, the local market and economic conditions, and the impact of the environment on our clients and our business at the time. More importantly, I do my homework around the local culture, read materials in advance, spend time at the Deloitte Touche Tohmatsu Limited (DTTL) member firm office and with the people in the local area, either through videoconference or face-to-face, to talk through any issues in advance. After I arrive at the DTTL member firm office or client site, it is important that I spend time with our people outside the work environment, perhaps over dinner, to capture the local culture, to get to know individuals personally.
—Deborah DeHaas, Vice Chairman and Central Region Managing Partner, Deloitte LLP

Various forms of intelligence can have a profound influence on organizational behaviors and outcomes, particularly in the area of leadership performance in a global environment. A review of the literature shows that over the last decade there has been new or renewed interest in diverse types of intelligences, such as cultural intelligence (for example, Kok-Yee and Earley[1]); emotional intelligence (for example, Mayer and Salovey[2]); practical intelligence (for example, Sternberg[3]); and social intelligence (for example, Goleman[4]).

Each of these streams of literature typically deals with one specific facet of intelligence. Our premise, in contrast, rests on the belief that it is the amalgamation of these facets that constructs the optimal leader profile in today's complex environment. This chapter deals with the various forms of intelligence that, in and of themselves, could predict strong leadership performance but when synthesized with the other forms of intelligence, can heighten the strength and success of the leaders assigned to manage across multiple geographies. We will discuss each of these forms of intelligence in more detail.

COGNITIVE INTELLIGENCE (IQ)

Cognitive intelligence as measured by the intelligence quotient or IQ has long been a hallmark of great leadership. Our experience with leaders who have been successful indicates that intelligence does factor into a person's level of competence. The question is, "How much intelligence do leaders need and in what particular areas?" In writing this book and talking with and observing successful leaders, there was one indisputable fact that emerged: cognitive intelligence matters and it is, in fact, a prerequisite for leaders and leadership. Thus we will cover some key concepts related to this type of intelligence and ways to assess executives and managers to make sure that they have the cognitive intelligence required to lead a global company.

Most authorities consider "superior" intelligence to be about an IQ of 130.[5] We see very few companies assess for IQs or ask people for their IQ or SAT scores (which are roughly correlated with IQs) when they are hiring and promoting talent. Assessing talent in general seems to be a prerequisite that is lacking. This led us to question how companies ensure that they have procured the intellectual know-how to outperform and keep outperforming the competition. Factors of intelligence become even more important in a global organization.

Justin Menkes, a leading authority in the field of evaluating C-suite executives, argues, "Executive intelligence is a distinct set of aptitudes that determines one's success in the three central contexts of work: the accomplishment of tasks, working with and through other people, and assessing/adapting oneself."[6] Malcolm Gladwell, author of *Outliers*, says that cognitive intelligence is only one factor in one's success.[7] He asserts that just because someone has a high IQ does not necessarily mean that he or she will be a "top-flight" executive. In fact, he argues that, at a certain point, cognitive intelligence becomes marginal. A few more points on the IQ test will not make much of a difference. It is the circumstance and the experience that one has that make the critical difference. Gladwell argues that it is focus and practice that make people exceptional. In his studies he has demonstrated that exceptional people in their field have at least 10,000 hours of practice to put them at the top of their game.

Merriam-Webster's defines *intelligence* as "the ability to learn or understand or to deal with new or trying situations; . . . the skilled use of reason; . . . the ability to apply knowledge to manipulate one's environment or to think abstractly as measured by objective criteria (as tests)." The critical question is not "how important is cognitive intelligence in success" but rather "how much intelligence is important?" At what point does it no longer make a difference? How does one assess executive intelligence? How do you develop raw talent—your leaders of the future who have graduated from good schools or who have good grades and high IQs—early so that they hone their ability to reason in a global context?

It has been widely asserted that a person's IQ, while important in providing an estimate of cognitive intelligence, can only go so far. Intelligence tests may measure the ability to retain knowledge and not necessarily the ability to succeed in the future. Some writers have argued that past performance is not necessarily a predictor of future success. As noted by Malcolm Gladwell, for example, successful people with high IQs are differentiated by practice in their field. The Beatles practiced over 10,000 hours before they perfected their music and Bill Gates had the opportunity to practice in a computer lab before anyone else did, and by doing so, gained invaluable experience that put him ahead of the competition. Gladwell has also noted that in some eras, leaders have the opportunity to be more successful than in other eras, for example, during the Industrial Revolution. Likewise, when you were born can have a direct effect on your success. For example, Steve Jobs, Scott McNeally, and Eric Schmidt were all born in 1954 and 1955 when the computer was in its infancy and they were able to take their knowledge and expand it at the right time. They had the opportunity and ability to adapt, listen, and build relationships, were open to alternative ways of doing things, and were flexible in how they approached strategy and planning. These points were the true differentiators, not the level of their IQs.

In his book *Talent on Demand*, Peter Cappelli underscores the importance of leadership development.[8] He notes that early industrial companies hired talent from top schools based on cognitive intelligence, but they also engaged this talent in extensive training and development to mold them into seasoned, effective leaders of the future. Cappelli's research shows that even with strong intelligence factors and development, leaders are not always successful and they must constantly be assessed to ensure that they are adapting, growing, and developing. Justin Menkes would agree with this but would add that current assessment techniques, largely based on past performance and behavioral interviews, are not sufficient to determine the long-term potential of a smart leader.

GE is not only known for developing top-flight leaders but also has served as a source of CEOs for companies in a wide variety of industries.[9] GE looks for both the intelligence factor and for what Jack Welch calls "the ability to look around corners and see what is coming and anticipate what to do."[10] The other critical factor is their ability to learn. At GE, this quality is defined as the ability to take on new experiences, understand them, listen to what is going on around them, and adapt to the environment in reasoned and constructive ways.

Maria DiPietro, a very successful global operations leader for GE, has characterized GE's efforts to develop its talented employees "being able to learn" in the following way: "You are thrown into different circumstances early in your career, and you have to figure out how to make sense of these circumstances and lead your team through them so they can achieve the results required. These 'stretch assignments' are what help you adapt and learn. They teach you to rely on others and to listen because you can't know everything about a situation. Once you get through one set of challenges, GE throws you into the next bigger assignment and sees if you can learn the dynamics in the new environment, and they keep doing that to ensure you learn and grow. It becomes second nature to a GE executive to become a learner."

In Gladwell's words, "Knowledge of a boy's IQ is of little help when you are faced with a roomful of clever boys."[11] The questions become: How do you develop this talent, keep it fresh, and ensure that you are selecting the right person for the global job ahead? Hewlett-Packard (HP) embarked on a rigorous internal study to discover what made people top talent and great leaders. Their research helped determine who was "best-in-class" as well as what it was that top leaders did that enabled them to develop their skills and superior performance.

Similar to GE, the great leaders who were role models early in their careers at HP had rotated into different and more challenging roles where they were out of their comfort zones. They had to develop and rely on new skills to make them successful. Every one of them had a strong people orientation. They were adaptable and flexed to the circumstances in which they found themselves. They were coaches to their people, and they were more concerned about their people and their careers than they were about their own careers. This research supports our findings that great transglobal leaders are also great on the people side of the equation and are adaptable. When we interviewed leaders from GE and HP who had large global roles, it became clear that they had to do a lot of listening.

In the words of Gary Budzinski, former senior vice president of HP: "I had to go around the world and listen to the issues from the right people. I had to take in information before I could come to any reasoned decisions. I had to understand the different values of the other parts of the world without compromising my own integrity. Listening helped me understand where people were coming from, and I could see the common threads that we could build on to move forward. Without this listening, I would never have been able to build the strong platform we operate from today."

Mark Hutchinson, head of GE China, puts it another way. He says he makes a point of regularly going to customers and forums in different parts of the world to just ask questions and listen to the responses: "This action has caused me to better understand the issues to change my own thinking and ultimately the direction we took. We made the right moves as a result. I think talking to people who don't think like you is important. It pushes your hypotheses and helps you see things differently—a critical element of being adaptable and flexible in a global world. You make fewer mistakes because you are able to factor in other points of view and you know what is acceptable in other people's minds, not just yours."

These comments clearly demonstrate that sheer cognitive intelligence is not enough; successful leaders also need people skills—that is, emotional intelligence.

EMOTIONAL INTELLIGENCE (EI)

We have made the case for cognitive intelligence as being important in a leader, but we have also revealed the critical necessity of the emotional and social intelligences in strengthening leaders' interpersonal and people skills. Mayer and Salovey define *emotional intelligence* as "the ability to perceive emotion, integrate emotion to facilitate thought, understand emotions, and regulate emotions to promote personal growth."[12]

In multicultural settings, the ability to identify with others' emotions and to understand them is the critical relationship bridge that connects individuals with diverse backgrounds and cultures. Jill Smart, chief HR officer of Accenture, states, "I manage both from my heart and my head." To Smart, making the emotional and social connection with her employees is important not just for building relationships but also more generally for guiding her decisions and giving her the framework to inspire and develop people.

Daniel Goleman popularized the model that views emotional intelligence as a wide array of competencies and skills driving leadership performances.[13] He outlined four main constructs relevant to leaders' emotional intelligence:

Self-awareness. The ability to recognize and understand one's emotions and their impact on decision-making ability

Self-management. The ability to control personal emotions and impulses and adapt to a different or changing environment

Social awareness. The ability to recognize and understand others' emotions

Relationship management. The ability to inspire, influence, and develop others while managing one's own emotions

Goleman subsequently expanded on the last two—the social intelligence constructs—to describe a leader's ability to interact effectively with others in any environment. These facets of intelligence, emotional and social intelligence, enable leaders to deal with ambiguity and diversity, both highly valuable assets in global settings. Since a great majority of this book deals with emotional intelligence, we haven't gone into it in depth in this section. You will find that we do so throughout the remainder of the book.

BUSINESS INTELLIGENCE (BI)

The 2008 financial meltdown and the tremendous focus on leadership have revealed the importance of business acumen in the global world of the future. A *New York Times* article (September 2009) discussed Ken Lewis, former CEO, president, and chairman of Bank of America. The article can be paraphrased as follows: Lewis grew up in the bank and was noted for his operational expertise. However, he lacked the broader fundamentals of leadership to pull the bank through a strategic crisis. The pundits referred to Lewis as a manager at best, certainly not a well-rounded leader. He lacked the strategic and transformational skills to guide the bank, and it became painfully apparent as the bank got deeper and deeper into crisis. Lewis had only one lens through which he viewed the business: the operational lens. This was the only lever he knew how to pull when times got tough.

While it could be argued that this is a skewed and an overly harsh portrayal of Ken Lewis, it brings attention to the notion that leaders often are too specialized and lack the experience in the full spectrum of arenas and functional areas necessary for success. We have seen this in other situations, as well, where companies have gone bankrupt because of the exclusive focus on financial engineering by the equity houses that have taken them over and left them highly leveraged. In the process, other critical aspects of operating a "whole company" that can sustain itself over the long haul were ignored.

Simmons Bedding Company is one that comes to mind as an example. Simmons, a long-standing, successful company that was privately held, succumbed to equity buyouts and proceeded down the long and painful spiral to bankruptcy. There are many other examples of leaders' using only one or two levers of a business to build profitability rather than building these organizations "to last," as defined by Collins and Porras.[14] Perhaps this is the key dilemma of business today: we do not have well-rounded leaders who understand the interplay of the various levers that drive an organization and when to pull what lever in order to sustain the organization over the long term.

When we reflect on leaders who have this ability, we naturally think of Jack Welch and his widely acclaimed and profitable run at GE for over 20 years. Welch, a PhD physicist, led GE through many different cycles with legendary performance. He was a master at operational excellence and spearheaded the Six Sigma method to streamline processes, improve performance, and enhance customer experiences. Welch often said he was the head of human resources and insisted that his leaders serve as chief human resources managers themselves. He understood how important the people factor was for any organization. He learned to leverage information technology to drive productivity and understood the power that technology would have in running the businesses of the future. He invested heavily in technology and insisted that his managers and leaders understand how to use technology appropriately to run their business.

Welch was one of the first to lead the way to outsourcing, which became a great lever in moving companies toward operating globally in a 24/7 environment. He was a CEO who understood the power of strategy, and he created a world-famous operating rhythm that yearly assessed and revised the company's strategy, looked at the people and how they stacked up against the strategy, and then evaluated the operation's performance and the financials. He knew the financial underpinnings of the GE conglomerate, but he also recognized the other key levers that had to work together to make the whole enterprise function smoothly and efficiently. Probably more than any other company, GE has developed and spun off many transglobal leaders to run major multinational companies successfully.

Research by Zack Hambrick, of Michigan State University, suggests that the personal and functional experience that leaders have shapes how they view and lead a company. If their experience is mainly through the financial track, they will approach their role from that perspective. If their framework and experience are through operations (as was the case for Ken Lewis), that is how they will approach their job. Carly Fiorina, former chairperson and CEO of Hewlett-Packard, had a strong marketing bent, and she spent much time trying to promote a sleepy tech company and make it sizzle. The press and others in the know say that this was ultimately one of the causes for her undoing.

In the past and in a less complicated world, leaders could function with a single-lens view; today and in the future, as businesses become more complex and global, leaders will have to access multiple lenses through which to understand and evaluate their companies, shape sustainable strategies, and drive results. The MBA with only a strong finance background will no longer be up to the task. Facing new challenges, leaders will require broader experiences to equip them to balance the tensions between the need for efficiency and the need to grow. Said differently, they will need to balance short-term results and long-term strategy.[15] In fact, many business schools and companies are assessing the models they are currently using to train leaders and finding them woefully insufficient. We contend that this has led to a short-sighted focus for many companies and the "achievement of goals at all cost" mentality that we have seen in the financial institutions. This type of behavior is what breeds a business culture that lacks integrity.[16]

Such a perspective can only underscore the negative elements that come into play when companies focus solely on financial results at the expense of other aspects, such as leader behavior and overall organization performance. When a leader has only one lens—the financial—with which to look at organization performance, the answers to all strategy questions are to "cut costs," and that usually means laying off people. Leaders with strong business intelligence, on the other hand, look at ways to improve profitability and reduce operations by leveraging technology, training people to improve process, setting clear metrics beyond financials, and so on. Those leaders who are successful over the long term know how to assess their organizations on multiple fronts and how to align them around key priorities to fuel growth.

To lead sustainable companies, in addition to broadening their focus beyond mere financials, leaders must now understand systems, marketing, sales, human resources, R&D, and operations. They have to become lead strategists, communicators, and marketers both internally and externally to customers and investors. The need for leaders to develop a broader understanding of business and organizations has been recognized by, incorporated into, and advocated by various models of leadership and organizational behavior including the Malcolm Baldrige approach[17] to quality and the McKinsey 7S Framework.[18]

Drawing on the literature, we have identified five key components of, and questions to ask in assessing, business intelligence:

> **Business strategy.** Do the leaders have the ability to develop and communicate a well-reasoned strategy for the business that everyone can understand? Can they delineate a strategy that guides action, provides a line of sight for employees at all levels, and serves as the basis for organization decision making and prioritization?
>
> **Customer focus.** Are current and future customer requirements understood and factored into business decision making? Do leaders have a keen understanding of key customer drivers?

Process management. Are processes aligned and integrated to deliver the expected results seamlessly and flawlessly in response to customer demands? Do the leaders have working knowledge of the processes that support the business and how they work?

Data and information. Are sufficient and timely data and information used by leaders to evaluate the performance of the business?

Human resources. Are leaders and their people knowledgeable and skilled enough to deliver on the strategy today and in the future? Do leaders have a deep understanding of the skills required to take the business into the future? Are there plans in place to continue developing the skill sets of current and new employees?

If these levers are aligned, the results should be forthcoming in the areas of financial performance, customer loyalty and satisfaction, employee retention and engagement, and quality of suppliers.

The leaders we interviewed know that results are more than just financial. While financial results are important to them—they are your entry into the game—these leaders also care intimately about employee engagement surveys and retention rates of top talent. They hold their managers accountable for creating a positive organizational culture and work environment, and they put plans in place to ensure that action is taken throughout the year to address workplace issues. The other outcomes they watch carefully are customer retention and loyalty, market share, and adaptation to new business and market trends. Successful leaders know they cannot sustain their businesses over the long term without achieving customer satisfaction and loyalty and delivering to future demands.

Inherent in being customer focused is ensuring that you have superb supplier quality so that you are delivering to your customers what they expect. Here is some great insight from Steve Sargent, president and CEO of GE Australia and New Zealand, from when he was a Six Sigma leader at GE Capital. He used to say that customers do not care if the product they are leasing from you did not come from the supplier on time. If the product is late and the customers can't get their business done because of your late delivery, they look to you from whom they leased the product. They care that you committed to having that product to them on a certain date, and if your supplier could not deliver, that was your problem, not theirs.

The point here is that effective global leaders take a holistic view of their organizations, measure and track critical aspects of their business beyond the financials, and hold their leaders accountable for these results as well.

Many of the leaders we interviewed expressed that (1) they can't have great companies without great strategies, (2) great strategy must have great customer intelligence as its underpinnings, (3) they can't deliver on the strategy unless they have the talent to do so, and (4) the talent can't be great if there are flawed processes and technology that undermine their efforts and make it impossible for people to get the information they need to do their jobs or to have development opportunities to grow. These leaders also know that it is great leadership at the end of the day that makes the true difference in the overall performance of the company. Thus, they take a holistic view of their organizations, know the set of lenses they need to look through to drive performance, and understand the levers they need to improve in order to stay on top of the game and deliver outstanding global results. They are continually using these lenses to adjust their strategy and to explain to people how the system all fits together to attain results.

The leaders we surveyed worked in multiple functions, businesses, and locations frequently throughout their careers. They were innate learners and were inquisitive about others. While these points are not particularly startling and the literature is replete with examples and frameworks to broaden leaders' thinking, the global arena is forcing leaders to think more broadly about the business intelligence quotient than ever before. The more leaders move about, the more they realize that more has changed and is different than remains the same or is common. As a result, pitfalls are difficult to anticipate and sidestep, but leaders who can avoid them become valuable human and business assets.

CULTURAL INTELLIGENCE (CI)

For aspiring transglobal leaders, one element that will be critical to their success is cultural intelligence. "*Cultural intelligence* refers to a person's capability for successful adaptation to new cultural settings, that is, for unfamiliar settings attributable to cultural context."[19] Adapting is multidimensional. Cultural intelligence is not just about being able to identify or spot the subtle differences between cultures but rather, it entails interpretation and making an appropriate response.

Understanding the cultural context in which work is being done is essential. Without cultural intelligence, leaders are walking through minefields never knowing when a bomb is about to explode or even if a bomb is there to begin with.

Here are some poignant examples of issues confronting leaders as a result of these cultural minefields:

- The manager who, soon after arriving in China, banned all forms of gift giving, seeing it as a form of bribery. He did not want to violate the firm's ethics policy. The manager failed to see *guanxi* for what it really is—a gesture designed to build relationships and develop bonds that are so necessary in China to do business successfully.

- The manager in Indonesia who interpreted a subordinate's inability to look his boss in the eye as a sign of dishonesty. He failed to realize that the subordinate saw avoiding eye contact as an act of respect.

- The Dutch CEO who was more comfortable standing just less than a meter away from his local team members in Brazil. He found himself being regarded as aloof and hard to get to know. His subordinates were used to standing less than half a meter apart when conversing with colleagues.

- The Swedish marketing director who initially interpreted her smiling Thai staff as motivated and happy. She was unable to discern the meanings of the nearly 20 different smiles in Thai culture. She didn't know that the smile *yim thang nam taa* ("I'm so happy I'm crying") is different than the smile *yim yaw* ("I told you so") or the smile *yim thak thaan* ("You go ahead and propose it, but your idea is no good").

- The high-driving project manager from Hong Kong used to getting action and results by shouting instructions to his loyal staff. He found himself chased with a machete when he carried on this practice in Indonesia.

- The new global CFO who, during revenue outlook calls, took many months to come to terms with the British controller who understated emerging difficulties, the Dutch controller who gave little color but was brutally blunt with the facts, the American controller who was overly optimistic, and the Japanese controller who continually understated the likely position.

- The U.S. CEO from the Southwest who, on his first overseas appointment, continued his open door and friendly policy that had (in his view) made him successful. Within two months in the new job, he had invited over a dozen executives to his home, some from a lower level within the organization. He was never slow in asking a broad range of people their opinions on the varied issues he saw confronting the organization. In doing so, he was inadvertently breaking down the power structure that was the foundation on which the organization ran. He was seen by many as incapable of making decisions and of trying to undermine his direct reports.

- The Singaporean CEO recently appointed to head a newly merged global company who decided to get 20 of the French and Asian executives together at INSEAD in France for a one-week, preintegration strategy meeting. When they broke for lunch on the first day, she was horrified to find wine being served for lunch and the French executives' partaking. She asked for it to be removed from subsequent lunches, not realizing the offense that would be taken.

- The Australian HR director who, in a global role when interviewing candidates for a European position, seemed to place no importance on the two degrees a very qualified French candidate had from one of the *grandes écoles* in Paris. The candidate withdrew her application believing her status would not be appropriately recognized if she took up a job in that organization.

- The new Dutch country head in China who announced to his subordinates: "I call a spade a spade. You will get a direct and honest answer from me, and I expect the same from you." When it became obvious that two of his subordinates were not working well together, he got them in his office and proceeded to get all the issues "on the table"; the next day, both resigned. He had not realized that the Chinese tend to avoid direct confrontation and prefer to work out issues subtly on a one-on-one basis.

- The CEO from Texas who wanted to sell his company to a European company and took the European leaders to a "gentleman's club" thinking that is what they would like. The Europeans were completely appalled by the behavior, and they had an uncomfortable evening. The Europeans did not know how to respond and found the Texan rude. The deal was never pursued.

These are just some examples of the many situations executives find themselves in every day as they move into new and challenging locations and confront new cultural mores and practices.

Psychologist Ronald Rohner defined *culture* as the totality of equivalent and complementary learned meanings maintained by human populations, or by identifiable segments of a population, and transmitted from one generation to the next.

Geert Hofstede, probably the most widely quoted authority on the topic of culture, referred to it as "collective programming." More recently, Hofstede coined the phrase "software of the mind."[20]

A culture is made up of shared attributes and rules that have been taught and passed down to members since childhood and continue to be transmitted throughout life by peers, the media, and colleagues. Many of these are unstated practices that are expected by the group, and often they can be picked up only by observation and personal immersion. Culture is not in our DNA. It is developed within the context of the culture we develop in. It is different from human nature and personality.

Even though there may be a dominant culture within a country, country and culture are not synonymous, and it is quite common that subcultures will exist within geographic or political borders. Individuals also develop personal cultures that evolve as a result of life experiences. These stored experiences influence their sense of identity, their worldview, and how they make sense of the interactions, situations, and challenges they face daily. Because individuals do not have the same exact life experiences, people develop unique personal cultures.

Nonetheless, there are attributes, values, and behaviors common to many cultures. J. Q. Wilson argued that there are four moral anchors that appeared throughout all cultures: fairness, sympathy, duty, and self-control. In fact, with globalization, the Internet, and mass media, there is a growing number of things that are understood by and becoming common to many cultures. Equally, many aspects of a culture can remain idiosyncratic, and there is little evidence that this will change.

Have you ever walked into a gathering where everyone, in an instant, knows you are "not from around here"? Within seconds, people can pick up and process hundreds of observations about someone new, and it is not long before the "outsider" barrier goes up. Looking and acting differently make it hard to communicate and be understood. We are all perceived, and we perceive, differently. In fact, some concepts, ideas, and behaviors are so subtle that only someone from that culture can understand them. Most people perceive their own culture as "normal," "good," or "the way it should be," and they view what is different in other cultures as "foreign" and, therefore, "bad."

Even staying at home can thrust you into a new culture. After a career at IBM, moving to Google may mean significant cultural adjustment in the same way a move from Singapore Airlines to Virgin Atlantic Airways or from the government to the private sector will. Organizations have their own cultures that have been passed down and developed over a long period. While these may be subtly refined and modified, such changes are usually minute when compared to the cultural foundations that form an organization's base.

P. Christopher Earley and Soon Ang describe cultural intelligence as consisting of three aspects: cognitive, motivational, and behavioral.[21] The *cognitive aspect* refers to the individual's ability to know what is happening in a given situation. The *motivational aspect* refers to the individual's willingness to act on what has happened. The *behavioral aspect* refers to the individual's ability to respond "appropriately and effectively."

"The challenge . . . is that in highly novel cultures, most of the cues and behaviors that are familiar may be lacking, so entirely new interpretations and behaviors are required. A person who is able to generate such new and appropriate responses has a high cultural intelligence."[22]

Leaders with high levels of CI have an ability to understand what is happening in a new environment without being held back by norms, ideas, or learned behavior from their own or even other cultures. They have the ability to let go of preexisting notions around why other people act the way they do. Rigid views of right and wrong, appropriate and inappropriate, better or worse, and acceptable and unacceptable all need to be viewed in the cultural context in which they occur; that cannot be done if one is deeply and rigidly entrenched in one's own views.

By suspending such entrenched views, leaders with high CI are able to interpret what is being communicated as if they were a member of that culture, and by doing so, they are able to act appropriately for the new cultural context. One critical element that cultural intelligence and emotional intelligence share is, as psychologist Daniel Goleman explains, "a propensity to suspend judgment—to think before acting."[23] This is important because "people don't care what you know, until they know you care."[24] Cues, hints, and gestures, inclinations, if viewed only through tinted glasses, can invariably mean that individuals may get it wrong, and this can play out in their interpretations and responses. Even if leaders can let go sufficiently to understand what is going on, this does not equate to having an adequate level of CI. Rather, leaders must accept that they need to engage with the culture and adapt to it. Only when their adaptation is followed by their appropriate behaviors can leaders be said to truly have a high level of cultural intelligence.

This success, determined by the ability to identify what is happening, motivate oneself to be adaptive, and to respond appropriately, can be transposed across cultures. That is why executives with high levels of CI are so mobile and capable of "hitting the ground running" in a wide variety of assignments across numerous companies, countries, and cultures.

A lot of research has been done over the years to try and qualify the traits, skills, and competencies of individuals who possess a high CI and as a result perform exceptionally well when working across cultures. Many predictors of cross-cultural success have been identified, and "cultural shock inventories" and cultural competency assessment measures have been developed to measure intercultural effectiveness. While it can be argued that there is no universal set of competencies and that leaders can be successful without high levels of the identified competencies, many would agree that success lies in the ability to blend competencies and reconcile them as leaders are called on to understand and cope with everyday cultural challenges and interactions.

One of the leading studies on the topic of cross-cultural leadership is reported in the book *Culture, Leadership, and Organizations: The GLOBE Study of 62 Societies.*[25] The GLOBE (Global Leadership and Organizational Behavior Effectiveness) Research Project involved 160 social scientists and management scholars from 62 cultures engaged in a long-term study of cross-cultural leadership. After 17,000 interviews, the project identified six "global leadership dimensions" that distinguish effective and ineffective leadership in various cultural settings:

- Charisma and/or values-based

- Team-oriented

- Self-protective

- Participative

- Humane

- Autonomous

The only one that received positive endorsement by all cultures was the charismatic and/or values-based leadership dimension, with scores ranging from 4.5 to 6.5 on a 7-point scale. The study also revealed that all the 62 countries investigated had varying degrees of nine "cultural dimensions":

- Power distance
- Institutional collectivism
- Gender egalitarianism
- Uncertainty avoidance
- In-group collectivism
- Future orientation
- Humane orientation
- Assertiveness
- Performance orientation

Other universal leadership values they identified were the following:

- Being trustworthy, just, and honest
- Having foresight and planning ahead
- Being positive, dynamic, encouraging, and motivating; building confidence
- Being communicative and informed; being a coordinator and team integrator

Several specific competencies have been commonly found in leaders with strong CI who could successfully operate across cultures (see Table 3.1). No leader had them all to the same degree, and only a few individuals possessed them all. Nonetheless, to be

Table 3.1   Competencies Relevant to Cultural Intelligence

Personal Competencies		Social Competencies
Curiosity	Open-mindedness	Social skills
Optimism	Positive self-image	Empathy and respect
Flexibility	Resilience and persistence	Metacommunication skills
Self-confidence	Nonjudgmental attitudes	Respect and positive regard for others
Positive attitude to taking risks	Goal-setting mindset	Open-mindedness to new ideas, new people, new places, and change
Tolerance for ambiguity and an ability to balance paradox	Ability to view self from the perspective of others	Open-mindedness to regular personal feedback from others
Positive attitude to self-development and learning	Ability to multitask with activities and people	

successful, one would need a reasonable level of the great majority of these competencies, which have been identified in many studies.[26]

Success also has a strong correlation with competency in learning a foreign language. Competency in a given technical or professional area is also extremely important, as one needs to more than hold one's own early on in a posting. Highly successful leaders are also self-aware to the extent that they can switch off homegrown habits, behaviors, or characteristics that they realize could affect how they are perceived or judged or that they think would confuse others. As Bill Berbach, joint founder of the DDB advertising agency, put it, "Whereas the writer is concerned with what he puts into his writing, the communicator is concerned with what the reader gets out of it."

Leaders with high CI also tend to be good mimics. There is an old saying: "People like people who like them." One could add in the global business context: "People like people who like them and are like them." Mimicry, whether it be by gestures, intonation, or space proximity, helps facilitate interaction. Even the use of silence can be mimicked.

High CI leaders also tend to be people who do not need constant gratification and positive feedback. This quality is important because some cultures are slow to praise, and when there is feedback, it may not be in the form one is used to, and it may not be positive. Successful leaders in a cross-cultural environment are resilient and persistent. They seek and accept all types of feedback, and they are appreciated and respected for doing so.

Transglobal leaders are likely to be managing a culturally diverse team of direct reports, and there is little evidence that this will change. CI is becoming a leadership competency that will be increasingly valuable and sought after.

GLOBAL INTELLIGENCE (GI)

Ranjay Gulati (the Jaime and Josefina Chua Tiampo Professor of Business Administration, Harvard Business School), when discussing the findings of our research, made the following point: "All successful leaders must have an acceptable level of competency in a range of universal leadership traits; without them their careers will be short-lived." But, he added, "That is not enough to operate successfully on a global stage, whether that stage is a group of countries spread across the world, a business line that spans many borders, or a multicountry regional job." Transglobal leaders need the competency in those universal traits, and they obviously need cognitive, emotional, business, moral, and cultural intelligences, but they need them all to operate in a multidimensional environment, and that's what most leaders struggle with.

Gulati is absolutely right. Sure, leaders need to be able to run and build teams, but transglobal leaders need to run diverse teams. Sure, all leaders need to be able to handle ambiguity ("I have some semblance of the context, but I'm not sure"), but transglobal leaders frequently need to operate and make decisions in the context of uncertainty ("I have no clue"). Sure, all leaders need a moral compass and within one national border, true north is true north, but using that compass across multiple borders means understanding that true north may not be simply found by reference only to the old tried-and-true, homegrown compass.

Global intelligence is an umbrella intelligence that one draws on to successfully execute one's job within a global context. The challenge transglobal leaders face is in developing strategy, structure, and operating mechanisms while maintaining a working balance between global standardization and local flexibility so as to generate an optimal result. This is always easier said than done given the different cultures, different legal and regulatory environments, different political systems, and the many other differences that impact doing business across the world. Invariably, those with good levels of global intelligence have honed their ability to make trade-offs to understand the validity of multiple points of view and ways of doing things, but in the end, they are able to make a decision that can be sold locally, regionally, and globally. As Gulati put it:

> The global leader is a bilingual and multidimensional translator able to communicate what headquarters is trying to do, what their goals are and why, and at the same time raising the sensibility of headquarters to the local environment. It's about having the team understand the context and the context understand the team.

Over the past two decades, every company has been impacted in some way or another by the wave of widespread globalization. Revolutionary advances in technology, large-scale mergers and acquisitions, breakthrough communication systems, and the ever-increasing ease and speed of transportation continue to make the world smaller while adding layers of complexity to the leadership development process. More and more leaders are being asked to organize global structures, build and maintain global technology platforms, and manage across multiple boundaries. Issues such as intellectual property rights, security, maintenance of technology platforms, antiterrorist protections, and the threats posed by hackers are now looming large in the world and greatly impact the business environment and organizations' ability to succeed at the global level. Legal departments are revising and fortifying their compliance procedures for worldwide application. Publicly traded companies are installing expensive governance structures and large-scale, enterprisewide systems to ensure that their books measure up to the growing stringency of international regulations. Marketing departments are refreshing their brands to fit cultural moods and habits.

The global challenges that leaders may face can stem from a number of factors, including these:

- The degree and amount of cross-border work that is required

- The complexity of a company's strategy and its business operations

- The comfort of the leaders and their understanding of the economic, social, and political landscape of the countries in which they are operating

- The leaders' desire to learn both the tacit and the expressed work rules of a group or society

There are many stories of expatriates feeling like "fish out of water" during the initial days of their assignments because they were unprepared for the global business context of where they were trying to implement a business strategy. Here is an example of these challenges:

A U.S. leader of a Fortune 500 global technology company made a substantial investment in several hundred acres of land in rural India. It was a joint venture with the state government with the purpose of developing the property into a high-tech "cybervillage." A lack of proper knowledge of the government operations and the bureaucracies of the construction system resulted in a gross underestimation of the time frames for completing the project. The project would have generally taken less than a year to launch and under three years to complete in the United States, but in India, it took multiple years just to acquire the requisite permits to initiate construction. The unexpected and costly delays ultimately forced the company to sell the property and abandon the venture.

Some people believe that the globalization of business will eventually result in a completely different legal, political, and economic infrastructure—that is, in an entity larger than and different from the laws, politics, and economic systems of any one nation. They believe that the operations of global corporations will become more similar than different and that a global managerial culture will emerge. Others believe that the historical, legal, political, and economic frameworks underpinning the country of origin will maintain the greatest influence over the operations of an organization, regardless of globalization. Regardless of which prognostication is correct, the implications for global managers are the same. They must be able to adapt and change what they do best in response to the context of the situation. Although it is uncertain how the infrastructure will ultimately play out, transglobal leaders must have a strong understanding and knowledge of how business is conducted in the country or countries in which they operate.

Deborah DeHaas, vice chairman and central region managing partner of Deloitte LLP, believes strongly that you need to make the investment in understanding the local operations and work habits of people on the ground. "You need to build sustaining relationships, walk in others' shoes, and understand them on their local turfs. Even reports and presentations sometimes don't make complete sense until you get an on-the-ground interpretation. We communicate so frequently over e-mail, which at times can be quick or terse. English is a particularly challenging language, and some things just don't translate well, particularly in a global environment where you can run the risk of misinterpretation or of not being able to build relationships across borders."

According to Dalton, Ernst, Deal, and Leslie, leaders who possess global intelligence will act in the following ways:

- Create an innovative corporate culture to leverage unique, culture-based knowledge and information for new product and service development.

- Conduct cross-cultural negotiations effectively.

- Make deliberate choices about how to conduct business successfully in a given part of the world.

- Apply knowledge of public regulatory frameworks in multiple countries.

- Discern and manage cultural influences on marketing and business practices.

- Understand how culture influences the way people express disagreement.

- Use cultural differences as a source of strength for the organization.

- Integrate local and global information for multisite decision making.

- Negotiate effectively in different business environments, even with jet lag and through translation.[27]

MORAL INTELLIGENCE (MI)

Everyone knows right from wrong. The challenge for some leaders is not the knowing but the doing. One of the results of the global financial crisis has been an incredible loss of trust in leaders, in institutions, in regulators, and in governments. Many leaders were seen to be self-serving and to be equating what was legal with what was right. Some of these leaders were morally corrupt; others, totally corrupt.

Even before this crisis, trust was a scarce commodity. Robert F. Hurley, professor at Fordham University Graduate School of Business, surveyed executives in 30 countries and found that roughly half of all managers didn't trust their leaders. The situation is even worse when it comes to CEOs. The Edelman Trust Barometer tracks the credibility of CEOs as spokespersons for their companies. In 2009, only 29 percent of respondents (ages 35 to 64) viewed information from the CEO as credible in 18 of the 20 markets surveyed. Credibility of information from CEOs is now at a six-year low at 17 percent, with new lows having been reached in South Korea, the United Kingdom, France, and Germany.[28]

One challenge for transglobal leaders is that they get a lot more latitude when it comes to trust from their own or from their tribe, but when they cross borders and cultures, they are outsiders and often feel that "trusting people not like us is hard." Trust has to be earned, and in the earning, a leader's words, deeds, actions, and interactions are watched 24/7. Very little escapes notice as the picture of whom and what the leader is and stands for is compiled.

To successfully establish and maintain trust, transglobal leaders need a high level of moral intelligence.

In their book *Moral Intelligence*, Doug Lennick and Fred Kiel define it as "the mental capacity to determine how universal human principles should be applied to our values, goals, and actions."[29] They go on to say, "In the simplest terms, moral intelligence is the ability to differentiate right from wrong as defined by Universal Principles. Universal Principles are those beliefs about human conduct that are common to all cultures around the world."

Lennick and Kiel believe integrity, responsibility, compassion, and forgiveness are critical principles of morally intelligent people.

All the global leaders we interviewed cited the absolute importance of such things as integrity, building trust, and having a moral compass that can help them navigate the ethical issues with which they are consistently confronted. They talked about black, white, and grey areas, and they also talked about issues of governance and ethics that were cloaked in local business practices, cultural nuances, and relationships.

Steve Bertamini, an American who first came to Asia with GE and who held many roles there, including the company's chairman of Northeast Asia, talked about the "GE way" as a guiding beacon that supplemented his own moral compass: "At GE, how you did it was as important as what you did." In Asia, Bertamini said, "We had zero tolerance. In fact, I think our ethics, if anything, were tougher here, regardless of local business practices. We wanted our customers and employees and the government to know what our values were and that we were very serious about them." Bertamini, now group executive director and chief executive officer of global consumer banking for Standard Chartered Bank, said, "It was tough leaving GE, but in Standard Chartered Bank, I have found another multinational with strong values and high ethical standards that align with mine and that makes being a leader a lot easier."

Your moral compass has, at its core, your values and beliefs, and as you grow and hone these, they become more integral to who you are, and they underpin those principles we talked about earlier: integrity, responsibility, compassion, and forgiveness. The more integral they become, the more they directly align to your behavior and, as a consequence, your reputation. Thus, your character eventually manifests itself into your reputation:

- What you are known as
- What you are known by
- What you are known for

As Jon M. Hunstman states in his book *Winners Never Cheat*, "It takes great courage to follow the moral compass in the face of marketplace pressure, but no challenge alters this fact: Regardless of who is holding the compass, or how they are holding it, or what time of the day it happens to be, north is always north and south is always south."[30]

For those core ethical issues that challenge your moral sense, issues transglobal leaders get faced with in the field, particularly outside of their home market, it is unacceptable and it is a cop-out to hide behind cultural smokescreens or excuses like "Everyone does it," "It's how business is done around here," or "If I don't do it, my competitors will."

Stephen Covey nailed it, saying, "From my experience in working with different people and cultures, I find that if certain conditions are present when people are challenged to develop a value system, they will identify essentially the same values. Each culture may express those values differently, but the underlying moral sense is always the same."[31]

Those universal human principles are common across cultures almost regardless of how a business, a business leader, or even the majority of local business leaders may choose to apply them. This is not to say that one does not need to recognize and show local flexibility around the fringes of those issues that arise which don't impact core values and beliefs. Additionally, the fact remains that across countries these universal principles are applied differently, may be prioritized in somewhat inconsistent ways, and reconciled differently when dilemmas arise. Thus, the sensitivity and adaptability discussed with respect to emotional, cultural, and global intelligence apply here. In this respect, as discussed in the next chapter, our survey showed that our 154 global leaders exhibited more flexibility than did those in the leader database we benchmarked.

The reputation of transglobal leaders, the extent to which they "walk the talk," and the experience their people have on the ground, will have profound impacts on the level of trust that is developed over time. Four common windows that are looked through to develop this view are reliability, openness, acceptance, and congruence (see Figure 3.1).

Today, more than ever, leaders have less time to build trust; communication is faster and multifaceted, quickly carrying interpretations of actions, deeds, and words all around the globe. In the absence of reliability and openness, mistrust and misunderstandings can quickly be ignited. But this rapidity of information diffusion and opinion formation can also work in the favor of transplanted leaders as new peers and employees seek information about them as leaders. This is particularly the case if they already have a reputation for integrity, responsibility, compassion, and forgiveness.

The more robust their moral compass and the more developed their moral intelligence, the more alignment leaders will display when it comes to their values, their beliefs, and their on-the-ground behavior. Their ability to be crystal clear regarding their

| Dependability
• Keeping promises
• Meeting deadlines
• Being on time
• Following through | **Reliability**

"I can trust her to . . ." | **Openness**

"I feel comfortable discussing this . . ." | Emotional Honesty
• Being generous with knowledge and information
• Being open about own views
• Showing candor
• Being honest about own limitations |
| Self-Other Orientation
• Caring about the impact on others
• Showing empathy
• Being nonjudgmental
• Accepting differences
• Valuing opinions of others | **Acceptance**

"I trust that he cares about . . ." | **Congruence**

"I can trust what he says . . ." | Credibility and Integrity
• Talking straight
• Being open with own agenda
• Making rules clear
• Walking the talk
• Acting authentically |

Figure 3.1 Trusting Relationships Improve the Quality of Client and Stakeholder Experiences

Source: Talentinvest, 2005.

personal moral compass and moral intelligence enables others to understand what is negotiable and what is not; this is essential for all leaders operating in global roles.

CONCLUSION

As we examined the literature and research on each of these forms of intelligence, it became increasingly clear that this foundation was too vast and that only a few could possess high levels of all forms of the intelligences described. This is why we call this the "foundation" and our "point of departure," because it informed the survey that we constructed to help tease out the "secret sauce" those really outstanding leaders possessed that made them successful. What aspects of these various intelligences really made a difference, and what were the areas that could not be ignored if leaders wished to truly have an impact at the global level? Thus, these intelligences became the foundation for our future discovery.

We started this chapter by saying that we do not believe that any leader can possess all of the intelligences required to be successful in the fast-paced and ever-changing global environment of today. We are not minimizing the importance of these aspects, but these alone will not ensure your success. You must have enough savvy, however, to realize all of the aspects that need to be considered as you venture forth in a global world. As you reflect on this chapter, you should consider the following questions:

- Do I have the necessary knowledge of the six intelligences to know what questions to ask and where to seek advice?

- Do I have a diverse group of thought leaders around me who can offer the context for the business I need to conduct?

- Do I understand my own biases so that I can listen to different approaches and contexts to help make the most reasoned decisions in a particular culture?

CHAPTER 4

What We Did,
Why We Did It,
and What We Learned

It is by logic we prove. It is by intuition we discover.
—JULES HENRI POINCARÉ[1]

To gain a better understanding of what we did and why we did it, it is worthwhile taking a few paragraphs to convey why the four authors were interested in the topic in the first place and the journey that brought them together.

The four of us had been on individual journeys in this area for many years, approaching the challenges of "leadership without boundaries" from slightly different angles. Our journeys crossed paths two years ago in Chicago, and we joined forces to pool our experiences and perspectives, conduct new research in the area of transglobal leadership, and then share our findings.

Linda Sharkey is a transglobal leadership consultant who formerly led the organization and leadership development functions at Hewlett-Packard and GE Financial. Linda learned very early in her career how rare effective and successful transglobal leaders were within organizations. "You couldn't just take your best and brightest, put them through an intensive development program, and confidently expect the majority of them to flourish in global roles outside their home country," Linda said. "My journey has focused on looking at the behavioral dimensions of successful leaders in global roles within those great companies where I worked."

Nazneen Razi, an HR practitioner who heads up HR at HCSC, the largest customer-owned healthcare organization in the United States, has held various global leadership roles. For eight years, she was head of Global HR at Jones Lang LaSalle, where she constantly scouted for global talent and repeatedly experienced acute shortages of successful multicultural leaders, irrespective of the business cycle. One of her greatest challenges was finding people to move into global assignments. "Too many of our managers and leaders, no matter how successful in their current assignments, just didn't meet the expectations the organization had for them in a global role." Nazneen continues, "A small number of these expatriates exceeded expectations, and I was curious to find out what made this exclusive group of individuals so unique and successful. If I could find the essence of an answer to that question, I could better respond to the growing daily requests from all corners of the organization, particularly in the emerging markets, for expatriate leadership talent to support our double-digit growth."

Robert Cooke, as lead researcher and now owner and CEO of Human Synergistics International, has spent his career studying leaders for client companies all over the world. He started to notice that research models and surveys that were appropriate for identifying and measuring effective leadership behaviors and strategies within a homogeneous cultural setting were not as useful as they could be for leaders working across multiple cultural contexts. "I started to hear more and more multinational clients asking for research-based tools that would help them to identify and develop in their leaders the qualities needed to be successful in global and multinational assignments," Rob said. "We needed new thinking and additional, specialized tools because so many clients and consultants were starting to request assistance in this area."

Peter Barge is an active director on a range of public and private company boards, and he is a private investor in a number of businesses in the Asia Pacific region. Peter had previously crossed over from the hotel industry to the real estate sector, where he was the CEO of a rapidly growing and successful real estate services company in the Asia Pacific region with over 16,000 employees in that region and 36,000 employees worldwide. Peter found in his CEO days that the greatest inhibitor to growth was the scarcity of leadership talent—especially in emerging markets. "I talked to CEO peers in Asia in other industries like IT, banking, and manufacturing, and we were all facing the same growth constraints. Too many high performers in their home countries were failing when we relocated them or when we asked them to take on regional roles required to support our growth. We all seemed to be in the same boat. However, I knew from my hotel days that it wasn't as big an issue in that industry, where for decades they seemed to have a far higher success rate in moving general managers and regional managers across the globe. I set out to learn why they were more successful," Peter said.

The four authors came to similar conclusions through different career journeys, and when their paths crossed in Chicago, it became clear that they were all looking for answers to the same basic questions. The prevailing leadership constructs seemed inadequate or incomplete in the context of the new challenges facing companies as they become increasingly more global. At that meeting in Chicago, they agreed that the overriding goal was to develop a better understanding of the factors that characterize effective transglobal leaders—that is, leaders who, according to Schon Beechler and Mansour Javidan, can influence individuals, groups, and organizations (within and beyond the boundaries of their own organization) that represent diverse cultural, political, and institutional systems in a manner that promotes the achievement of the global organization's goals.[2]

While the superordinate goal was fairly well shared by the authors, their professional and personal objectives around that goal were not necessarily consistent. That's probably what happens when four people with diverse backgrounds, roles, and interests get together to collaborate on any project. At worst, the differences are potentially grounds for ensuring that the project is never completed; at best, the differences maximize the likelihood that the project will actually produce results that are useful. The differences revolved around, for example, the dissemination and application of the results. More specifically, should the dimensions identified be used to select and place people into transglobal leadership positions, or should they be used to provide feedback to those already in such positions to facilitate their growth and development? Should the results be shared with others as they emerged, or should they be presented only at the end of the project after being fine-tuned? Similarly, should the findings, as they emerged, be presented in articles and at conferences, or should everything be put together into a book? We believe that these differences, along with others, including our qualitative versus quantitative orientations, though sometimes difficult to navigate, led us to a more useful and multifaceted outcome.

In general, we reconciled our different orientations by implementing multiple methods and procedures and by working toward multiple products that were complementary, mutually reinforcing, and responsive to our varied interests. Most importantly, we implemented research activities based on both qualitative and quantitative approaches, beginning with observations and interviews, moving on to surveys, and then returning to another round of interviews. With respect to sharing our findings, we decided to do so incrementally, primarily through presentations, and to use the feedback to strengthen this book. With respect to application, we decided to focus on both interviews that could be used for screening and selecting people for global positions and surveys that could be used to guide and promote their development. The only downside to this integrative approach was that conversations between dyads within the team focused, almost on a monthly basis, on whether or not we would ever finish this thing!

THE POINT OF DEPARTURE: READING, TALKING, AND AGREEING ON THE FOUNDATION

To get things going, we carried out informal interviews (more like discussions) with dozens of transglobal leaders and human resources executives responsible for international business. These preliminary interviews focused on the challenges that these leaders were facing as their organizations were expanding globally, the resources they relied on to help them identify and prepare leaders for global assignments, and the types of skills, qualities, and attributes they thought were relevant to success in global roles.

Possibly the most consistent and important takeaway from these interviews was that there was a critical need for research, information, and tools focusing on the factors related to the success or failure of people taking on transglobal leadership assignments. One after another, the executives reiterated that the acceleration in the globalization of their organizations was far outpacing the development of knowledge around selecting and developing the right types of leaders. We kept hearing that the existing literature on leadership, while appropriate for local leaders in certain countries, needed to be supplemented to better address the challenges of global positions. We also heard, time and time again, that mistakes were being made in selecting leaders for global assignments, that those mistakes could not be quickly corrected, and that the costs of such mistakes were enormous. Almost without exception, the executives we contacted strongly encouraged us to move forward with our research, expressed a willingness to help, and/or said that they would be interested in seeing our results.

With respect to the resources they relied on when dealing with transglobal leadership challenges, the executives mainly mentioned books. The first stream of books included those on cross-cultural issues and managing in different countries, books with which one or more of us were very familiar and deeply appreciated. These included Geert Hofstede's landmark work *Culture's Consequences*[3] and the societal values shaping organizations and management in over 60 countries; Edward T. Hall's writings *The Silent Language* and *The Hidden Dimension*[4] guiding meaning, customs, and behavior in selected American, European, and Asian countries; Charles Hampden-Turner and Fons Trompenaars's work *Riding the Waves of Culture*, delineating key dimensions of business behavior and four resulting types of corporate cultures[5]; Robert J. House's work (with Paul J. Hanges, Mansour Javidan, Peter W. Dorfman, and Vipin Gupta) on the impact of societal culture on organizational behavior and leadership in 62 countries[6]; and Terri Morrison, Wayne Conaway, and George Borden's guidebook *Kiss, Bow, or Shake Hands* on doing business in different places throughout the world.[7]

While we found these and related writings to be extremely informative and even fascinating, we really were not focusing on understanding and explicating the values and norms prevailing in specific countries. Similarly, our goal was not to prescribe specific ways of thinking and behaving that could help an executive fit in and easily interact with others while on assignment in a division located in one country versus another. Rather, we wanted to identify the ways of thinking and behaving that, more generally, would enable an executive to effectively lead a multinational team, coordinate with units located in a variety of different countries, and work productively in a new location regardless of the societal values prevailing in that country (for example, the degree of power distance, individualism versus collectivism, or uncertainty avoidance) and shaping the unit's culture.

Thus, we directed more attention to a second stream of books—those focusing on various types of intelligence and its offshoots. Based on what we were hearing, books and articles with the words *intelligence* or *quotient* in the title had become the go-to source for ideas and suggestions about transglobal leadership. We began by revisiting Daniel Goleman's *Emotional Intelligence*[8] and some of the more recent works he's published with coauthors. We also reviewed the original 1990 work on emotional intelligence by Peter Salovey and John Mayer and their approach to measuring it through tests (patterned after those designed to measure other forms of intelligence).[9] We then moved on to books and articles focusing on the other types of intelligence reviewed in Chapter 3— cognitive intelligence, business intelligence, cultural intelligence, global intelligence, and moral intelligence.

Writings on cultural intelligence seemed particularly relevant, including P. Christopher Earley and Soon Ang's *Cultural Intelligence: Individual Interactions Across Cultures*.[10] References on moral intelligence included books by Doug Lennick and Fred Kiel as well as Arthur Drobin.[11] Naturally, our review included many fine works without the words *intelligence* or *quotient* in the titles, including Ed Cohen's *Leadership Without Borders*;[12] Morgan McCall and George P. Hollenbeck's *Developing Global Executives*;[13] and the Center for Creative Leadership's *Managerial Effectiveness in a Global Context*.[14] Nevertheless, as shown in Figure 3.1, the intelligence facets served as our point of departure and provided us with a way of organizing our thoughts and generating a wide array of items for measurement purposes.

We then got busy dissecting the books and articles, as well as the minds of our colleagues and interviewees, to draft sets of survey items associated with each of the five types of intelligence. As we progressed, we noticed that we were leaning in the direction of behavioral items focusing on leaders' interactions with others, the choices and decisions they made for their units and organizations, and the way they approached their work. It was not at all clear that the "things" we were measuring exclusively represented intelligence in the traditional sense of the term (that is, the capacity for understanding and ability to perceive and comprehend meaning). Simultaneously, it became very clear that we were not building a test, at least not one of the "IQ" variety, that asks people to solve problems or provide answers to questions that can be scored as right or wrong.

We also noticed that many of the behavioral items we were developing were reminiscent of scales within personality indicators or personal styles inventories written many years before, or independently of, the books and tests assessing emotional intelligence. For example, some items seemed to correspond to the "agreeableness" and "conscientiousness" dimensions of the Five-Factor Model of Personality.[15] Others seemed to parallel the "humanistic-encouraging" scale of J. Clayton Lafferty's Life Styles Inventory[16] and the "emotional stability" scale of Raymond Cattell's 16PF.[17]

Simultaneously, as things progressed, it sometimes became difficult to identify ex post facto the particular type of intelligence that we had originally written specific items to measure. The boundaries between the five of the six facets of intelligence on which we eventually focused started to break down, and there seemed to be some common themes or dimensions cutting across them. Also, in the process of crafting an endless list of items to tap the many traits or attributes associated with each type of intelligence, it became painfully clear that the size of the resulting array or matrix of behaviors would likely far exceed the crisp and concise list that we had originally envisioned.

We had already agreed to not measure cognitive intelligence (the type of intelligence most commonly evaluated through IQ tests) for two reasons: (1) it is traditionally measured by tests rather than surveys, and (2) high cognitive intelligence is a basic entry requirement for effective leadership. We decided to use only the remaining five facets of intelligence—emotional, business, cultural, global, and moral—as our point of departure and to use the writings on them as a temporary framework for classifying the measurement items that we were developing. We tried to remain flexible and open to the possibility that our research could suggest a different organizing framework and possibly a better way to present the factors underpinning effective transglobal leadership. To that end, we began de-emphasizing the use of the words *intelligence* and *quotient* and temporarily gravitated toward the word *quantum* (even though, and possibly because, at that stage it wasn't really linked to the research or writings on transglobal leadership). In fact, the former words were rarely mentioned as we continued to interview leaders and began contacting potential respondents to the survey we were developing.

OUR SURVEY RESEARCH

We describe in the following sections the research and development activities we carried out to write the first versions of our survey and to identify the dimensions underlying transglobal leadership. These sections focus on things like our sample, the design of the survey, and some of the statistical approaches used to analyze the data. If you don't enjoy reading about research or you break out into a sweat at the mere mention of statistics, you might want to skim over some of these sections and focus more heavily on the "What We Learned" section later in this chapter.

Our Respondents

Over the years, the four of us had met a range of successful trans-global leaders working at many different levels of organizations in a broad range of industries and countries. Linda and Rob had the added advantage of serving as consultants to some of the top "most admired" companies in the world. One of the important things we decided to do was identify a sample of these leaders, and have them identify others, with a track record of global success—leaders who had "hit the ground running" when they were posted to new and challenging assignments in new countries or new businesses or when they were asked to take on regional or global roles. "We wanted to see what made this group tick, identify the behavioral dimensions that differentiated them from other leaders, and quantify their impact compared to that of leaders in general," Rob explained. With the benefit of Human Synergistics' leadership databases developed over 40 years that contained in-depth data on thousands of leaders, we set about to see if there were differences and what they were.

We hoped to survey about 150 leaders and interview a sub-sample of them. In the process of contacting the leaders we knew, a number of multinational companies heard about our study, and they informally agreed to participate and nominated some of their own leaders who had a high success rate internationally within their organizations. In many ways, the leaders in our sample were identified using a variation of what used to be called the "reputational" approach (dating back to Floyd Hunter's research in the 1950s on power[18])—asking informed people to name leaders who were successful in global assignments and who seemed to have what it took to work with people with diverse backgrounds. We believed that this approach would enable us to identify leaders who were, at best, exceptional and, at worst, above average in terms of effectiveness.

The leaders were then asked to provide us with direct and honest self-descriptions using our detailed survey made up of a battery of descriptive statements that potentially distinguished between what we began referring to as "global" versus "local" leaders. These leaders also were asked to nominate at least one other person who knew them well and could describe them in a parallel survey. (This was phrased as an option exclusively to embellish our study. And while we promised to summarize and report back the leaders' own responses, we were not going to provide any feedback based on the confidential surveys completed by others.) We also personally interviewed many of the survey participants and discussed their journeys, experiences, and leadership styles. Excerpts from these personal interviews are woven throughout the book to add color and depth to the survey results.

The final sample of 154 leaders represents over a dozen nationalities. Furthermore, the leaders ranged in age from 33 to 67, 34 percent were women and 66 percent were men, and all of them had held many and varied positions across more than 20 industries. Companies for whom the leaders worked included GE, HP, Baker & McKenzie, Standard Chartered Bank, Procter & Gamble, Jones Lang LaSalle, ANZ, Accenture, Accor, Genpact, and InterContinental Hotels, to name but a few.

THE SELF-REPORT SURVEY

We worked diligently on developing our Quantum Survey (now called the Transglobal Leadership Survey) by writing a series of statements that we believed would capture the behaviors associated with effective transglobal leadership according to our readings and interviews. We wrote statements that people could respond to using a 7-point scale with phrases at the endpoints. The phrase at one endpoint described a behavior that was descriptive of transglobal leaders while the phrase at the other endpoint described an opposing behavior. Our approach was inspired by Osgood, Suci, and

Tannenbaum[19]—though they used single words while we relied on phrases. We had what seemed to be a good set of items, particularly with respect to the phrases on the global leader side. The opposing phrases also were on target but tended to describe leaders who either wouldn't have a prayer in a global setting or would quickly alienate virtually everyone with whom they came into contact.

We fortunately made the quasi-scientific decision to pilot test the survey. We asked a few of the leaders whom we knew well to take the survey and give us feedback on it before sending invitations out to the larger group. That fortuitous decision ended up delaying our study by well over a month, but it saved us from administering a survey that we already feared was overly transparent, subject to social desirability effects, and too susceptible to "faking." More than a couple of our testers confirmed that the "right" answers were too obvious and that some of the "wrong" answers were so negative that relatively few respondents would dare to select them.

So we went back to the drawing board, or in this case, back to the Windows Publisher file containing our survey. We worked hard to modify the nonglobal statements and, whenever possible, make them descriptive of a leader who might be effective but only in a local rather than a global assignment. When this was not practical, we rewrote the local endpoint to be neutral or at least less negative than before. As a result, we were able to make the sets of descriptors somewhat more balanced and the local responses less undesirable. While many, if not most, of the global descriptors could still be easily discerned, at least we were no longer forcing respondents to choose those descriptors merely to avoid registering a strongly negative response. Table 4.1 presents 10 examples of the 71 self-report items.

We sent each of the transglobal leaders an e-mail to introduce our research and invite them to complete the survey. They were asked to click on a link and complete the Quantum Survey online. The link took them to an introductory page that is reproduced here as Exhibit 4.1.

Table 4.1 Examples of the Self-Report Survey Items

Left Item	1	2	3	4	5	6	7	Right Item
Base decisions on the organization's long-term strategy.	1	2	3	4	5	6	7	Base decisions on current opportunities, issues, and demands.
Proactively collect the type of information needed by my unit.	1	2	3	4	5	6	7	Reactively accept information (rather than seeking it out).
Expect others to redefine their roles in response to my work needs and expectations.	1	2	3	4	5	6	7	Redefine my role in consideration of the work needs and expectations of others.
Show faith and confidence only in people who are similar to me.	1	2	3	4	5	6	7	Show faith and confidence in people in general.
Respond to diverse and subtle expressions of disagreement.	1	2	3	4	5	6	7	Assume agreement unless others differ in a direct and overt manner.
Balance the needs for achieving global consistency and adapting to local norms.	1	2	3	4	5	6	7	Emphasize global consistency over local adaptation.
Live or die by the budgets that have been set.	1	2	3	4	5	6	7	Work with budgets in the context of the current business environment.
Emphasize rules, formal structures, and how things are supposed to work.	1	2	3	4	5	6	7	Emphasize norms, the informal network, and how things really get done.
Prefer continuity and stability in my work situation.	1	2	3	4	5	6	7	Don't need continuity in my work situation.
Emphasize the need to treat all customers the same.	1	2	3	4	5	6	7	Show sensitivity to different types of customers and their specific needs.

Exhibit 4.1 Quantum Edition of the Transglobal Leadership Survey

This is a new survey that will be used to help select, develop, and prepare managers for global leadership positions. As a successful global leader, your responses to this survey will help us to validate the measures and develop benchmarks against which future respondents' results can be profiled.

Your responses to this survey will be summarized and returned to you along with the combined results of other effective leaders. A summary report focusing on aggregated data will be provided to the various organizations involved in this project. All reports will maintain the confidentiality of individual respondents—and your honest and objective responses will maximize the usefulness of the results (and the survey) to your organization.

When you click on the **Next** button below, you will be presented with a series of windows, each of which includes pairs of statements focusing on your managerial styles and behaviors. The statements in each pair represent alternatives that might be descriptive of you. Compare the two alternatives, and decide which one more accurately describes your behavior as a manager. Then, select one of seven response options.

For example,

Left Statement								Right Statement
	1	2	3	4	5	6	7	
Make decisions based on people's feelings.	O	O	O	O	O	O	O	Make decisions on the basis of facts and figures.

If the **left** statement more accurately describes you, click on one of the three buttons to the *left* of 4 to indicate that your behavior

- 1 is **almost exactly like** the left statement.
- 2 is **much like** the left statement.
- 3 is **somewhat like** the left statement.

If the statement on the **right** is more accurate, click on one of the three buttons to the *right* of 4 to indicate that your behavior

- 5 is **somewhat like** the right statement.
- 6 is **much like** the right statement.
- 7 is **almost exactly like** the right statement.

(continued on next page)

Exhibit 4.1   Quantum Edition of the Transglobal
Leadership Survey *(continued)*

If **neither** alternative is more descriptive of you, click on the *middle*
button:

- 4 is **about equally like** the left and right statements.

After you have completed these questions, you will be asked to
describe your impact on the people around you, to provide some background information, and to nominate other people to describe you. Please
answer these questions and then click on the appropriate button to submit
your responses. Thank you for your participation.

Source: Adapted from Transglobal Leadership Survey—Quantum Edition. Copyright
2010 by Human Synergistics International. All rights reserved.

As requested in these instructions, after describing themselves,
the leaders were asked to describe the impact that they felt they had
on the behavior of the people around them. For this purpose, we
included in the survey 12 questionnaire items (as shown in Table 4.2)
from the Leadership/Impact Survey developed by Rob Cooke to
help leaders understand the type of culture they create and to redirect
their leadership strategies to have a more positive, constructive
impact.[20] We included these items because we felt that the leadership
styles we were measuring might enhance the effectiveness of leaders
not only directly but also indirectly via the organizational cultures
they created. We wanted to test this hypothesis.

The Leadership/Impact inventory in Table 4.2 measures the
impact of leaders in terms of the three sets of behaviors and cultural
styles described below.

A Constructive Impact and Culture Emerge
When Leaders . . .

- Encourage and enable organizational members to
  approach tasks and interact with others in positive ways
  that are consistent with personal needs for growth and
  satisfaction;

- Reinforce and inspire their subordinates (and others with whom they work) to demonstrate a balanced concern for people and tasks, focus on the attainment of both personal and organizational goals, and work to reach those goals through cooperative efforts; and

- Promote achievement-oriented, self-actualizing, encouraging, and affiliative behaviors throughout the organization.

Table 4.2 Leadership/Impact Survey Items

To What Extent Would You Say You Motivate or Drive the People Around You to . . . ?	1–5 "To What Extent" Response Options				
1. Assist others in solving work-related problems.	1	2	3	4	5
2. Cooperate with others.	1	2	3	4	5
3. Strive to be accepted and part of the "in-group."	1	2	3	4	5
4. Strictly adhere to policies and standard operating procedures.	1	2	3	4	5
5. Delay taking action until receiving clearances or approvals.	1	2	3	4	5
6. Keep their opinions and ideas to themselves.	1	2	3	4	5
7. Criticize current practices as a way to get their ideas accepted.	1	2	3	4	5
8. Aggressively assert themselves.	1	2	3	4	5
9. Turn their job into a contest.	1	2	3	4	5
10. Become preoccupied with details and unnecessary precision.	1	2	3	4	5
11. Take on challenging tasks with a sense of confidence.	1	2	3	4	5
12. Think in unique and independent ways.	1	2	3	4	5

Source: Impact items and style descriptions adapted from Robert A. Cooke and J. Clayton Lafferty, Leadership/Impact with permission. Copyright 1996 by Human Synergistics International. All rights reserved.

A Passive/Defensive Impact and Culture Emerge When Leaders . . .

- Compel and implicitly require organizational members to interact with one another in self-protective ways such that their personal security will not be threatened;

- Expect and reinforce others around them to emphasize people at the expense of tasks (for example, withhold negative, yet necessary, feedback), subordinate themselves to the organization (follow rules even when they're wrong), and play it safe rather than take reasonable risks that could enhance performance; and

- Promote approval-oriented, conventional, dependent, and avoidant behaviors throughout the organization.

An Aggressive/Defensive Impact and Culture Emerge When Leaders . . .

- Drive organizational members to approach tasks in forceful ways to protect their status and security;

- Reinforce and require their subordinates and peers to emphasize tasks and short-term performance (rather than the needs of people); narrowly pursue their own objectives over those of other members and units; and compete rather than cooperate; and

- Promote oppositional, power-oriented, competitive, and perfectionistic behaviors.

The items shown in Table 4.2 that we included in the Quantum (Transglobal Leadership) Survey can be broken down this way: items 1, 2, 11, and 12 measure a constructive impact; items 3, 4, 5, and 6 measure a passive/defensive impact; and items 7, 8, 9, and 10 measure an aggressive/defensive impact.

The Descriptions-by-Others Survey

While we all agreed that self-report inventories are invaluable, we decided as noted above that it would be useful to collect some parallel data on our leaders based on the judgments and reports of others. Thus we developed a Descriptions-by-Others version of the Quantum Edition of the Transglobal Leadership Survey, and we asked the leaders, upon their completion of the survey, to nominate associates to complete a similar survey:

> To ensure that this survey works properly, we need to compare managers' self-descriptions to the way they are described by others. Therefore, we would greatly appreciate it if you would provide the names (and e-mail addresses) of up to three associates who could describe you on a parallel form of this survey. The e-mail addresses you provide will be used only to invite your associates to participate in this project. Their responses will be used exclusively for research purposes and will not be reported back to you or anyone else.

Quite a few of our leaders took the extra step to provide us with the name and e-mail address of a person who could describe them. The others whom the leaders nominated were sent invitations to complete the survey, with assurances that their responses would be treated with confidentiality and used exclusively for research purposes. The survey they were asked to complete included the 71 behavioral items based on the intelligence quotient and related literature, the 12 items tapping the impact of the leaders, and 10 additional semantic differential items (shown in Table 4.3) focusing on the leaders' effectiveness.

The first 8 of the 10 semantic differential items were taken directly from the Leadership/Impact inventory. We included them in the Quantum Edition of the survey so that we could check to see if the leaders in our sample were, in fact, viewed by others as above average in effectiveness. While we anticipated that they would

Table 4.3 Descriptions-by-Others Survey

The two statements on each line below represent opposing viewpoints. Please check the box (1–7) that best represents your assessment of the manager you are describing.

	1	2	3	4	5	6	7	
Enhances others' productivity	1	2	3	4	5	6	7	Reduces others' productivity
Is relaxed and at ease	1	2	3	4	5	6	7	Is tense and stressed out
Is ready for promotion to a higher level	1	2	3	4	5	6	7	Is not ready for promotion at this time
Makes people feel empowered	1	2	3	4	5	6	7	Makes people feel micromanaged
Accepts feedback constructively	1	2	3	4	5	6	7	Reacts to feedback defensively
Brings out the best in people	1	2	3	4	5	6	7	Brings out the worst in people
Emphasizes long-term performance	1	2	3	4	5	6	7	Emphasizes short-term effectiveness
Interested in self-development	1	2	3	4	5	6	7	Not interested in self-development
Thinks globally	1	2	3	4	5	6	7	Thinks locally
Is best suited for an international role	1	2	3	4	5	6	7	Is best suited for a domestic role

Source: Adapted from Robert A. Cooke and J. Clayton Lafferty, Leadership/Impact. Copyright 1996 by Human Synergistics International. All rights reserved.

score higher than the average leader in the Human Synergistics data sets, we expected that there would be some variance in the effectiveness of the leaders in our Quantum Survey sample. We wrote the last two items expressly for this research, and we included the final one, in particular, to help us distinguish between the good versus great transglobal leaders.

Of the 154 transglobal leaders who completed the self-description form of the survey, more than half of them (79) were subsequently described by another person.

A Note on Statistics

We used a variety of statistical analyses to look at the data, with a heavy reliance on basic correlations and tests to check the significance of differences between mean scores for groups. We decided to look at the data in a more sophisticated way, using procedures that statisticians call *factor analysis* and *principal component analysis.* These techniques are used to identify the dimensions underlying variability or driving responses to large sets of questionnaire items. They are helpful in reducing data, delineating the basic factors that truly are being measured, and identifying the subsets of questions associated with each factor.

As a caveat, these types of analyses are typically used in heavy-duty academic studies leading to journal articles with lengthy titles, which usually include a colon and subtitle and at least a few indecipherable words. Additionally, the technique really works best with surveys when the researchers have collected data from numerous respondents. While we'll continue collecting data and use these techniques again on larger samples, we applied factor analysis with our initial sample to guide the next version of our survey and share our initial findings with others. In an exploratory mode, we applied principal components analyses with varimax rotation on the data file with our leaders' responses, the file with the descriptions by others, and even a combined file. Due to our small n, we interpreted the results cautiously and in consideration of other findings resulting from more basic statistical analyses.

WHAT WE LEARNED

We learned three major things about transglobal leadership over the past two years. The first and probably most important thing we learned is that it is not particularly meaningful to categorize all the different behaviors we were measuring into the five types of intelligence we considered provided the foundation for our research. Looking at the data, we simply did not see responses to the items associated with each particular type of intelligence hanging together. Instead, we learned that five new major dimensions cut through and, in a sense, defined the various behaviors we were measuring. These dimensions, along with three of the most important survey items associated with each of them, are given below.

Uncertainty Resilience

- "Reads" and analyzes ambiguous situations from multiple perspectives—as opposed to "reads" and analyzes ambiguous situations in a straightforward, linear way

- Deals with multiple people and/or situations simultaneously—as opposed to focuses on one person and/or situation at a time

- Interprets things loosely and figuratively—as opposed to takes things literally

Team Connectivity

- Is better at listening—as opposed to is better at talking

- Redefines her or his role in consideration of the work needs and the expectations of others—as opposed to expects others to redefine their roles in response to her or his work needs and expectations

- Can see the world through the eyes of others—as opposed to sees the world mainly in his or her own unique way

Pragmatic Flexibility

- "Bends" rules and values as required by the situation— as opposed to refuses to compromise on principles (including those that might conflict with local norms)

- Will "adjust" his or her personal values to get the job done—as opposed to maintains his or her personal integrity at all costs

- Works with and adjusts budgets in response to current business dynamics—as opposed to takes budgets seriously and lives within the constraints they impose

Perceptive Responsiveness

- Rewards people in "customized" ways, based on their needs and interests—as opposed to rewards people in "standardized" ways, treating everyone the same

- Shows sensitivity to different types of customers and their specific needs—as opposed to emphasizes the need to treat all customers equally and the same

- Sees negative feedback as an impetus for change and development—as opposed to uses negative feedback as a lever to get additional resources and support

Talent Orientation

- Gets involved in and drives succession planning initiatives—as opposed to sees succession planning as best driven by specialists in the HR department

- Carefully considers core business processes when discussing levers for improving performance—as opposed to stays away from the process details

• Uses people and human resources development as strategic levers—as opposed to uses technology and process as strategic levers

The first four dimensions were clearly identified by the analyses we described above. The fifth dimension, talent orientation, did not as clearly emerge statistically most likely due to the fact that we included just a few (rather than many) items focusing on this set of leadership behaviors. We note that this factor was repeatedly mentioned throughout the interviews we conducted. We believe that we will see this fifth dimension, and possibly others, emerge as we continue to develop our survey, administer it to more people, and reanalyze the data. In any case, the data and analyses pointed us in an entirely new direction for thinking about, classifying, and writing about the behaviors that enable certain leaders to excel in a global setting.

The second major thing we learned is that these five sets of behaviors are somewhat independent of one another and are not necessarily all displayed together or to the same degree by leaders in global positions. More technically, the analyses we carried out suggested that the behaviors are factors or dimensions rather than tendencies that naturally coincide and coexist. This means that in any given random sample of leaders, some will frequently exhibit all five behaviors, others rarely will exhibit any of them, and yet others will exhibit some of them but not all of them. Thus, it is possible that certain leaders are strong on, for example, uncertainty resilience and team connectivity but may rarely, if ever, practice the other three critical behaviors.

So, what does this mean from a practical perspective? Among other things, this finding suggests that in today's world people who actively practice all five sets of behaviors are somewhat of a rare breed. We may find that most people exhibit one or two of these behaviors; however, the number showing polished skills along all five dimensions is likely to be small. From a more positive perspective, this means that there is likely to be a good number of people in any given organization who exhibit three or four of the behaviors and can be groomed for global positions.

In terms of leadership development, this learning has at least three important implications. First, in any particular organization, we may find that some leaders have been surviving in, and perhaps performing moderately well in, transglobal leadership assignments. With respect to behavioral styles, their success may be due exclusively to their tendencies along one or two dimensions like uncertainty resilience and perceptive responsiveness. If so, we can potentially increase their effectiveness by systematically focusing development efforts on the remaining dimensions. By doing so, we can turn a moderately effective leader into a more effective, possibly great, global leader. Alternatively, we might be able to help that leader run a more successful business by encouraging and assisting him or her in building a leadership team that includes members who frequently exhibit the "missing" behaviors. Our intent was to help already successful transglobal leaders be even more successful.

Second, in terms of selecting leaders for global positions, this learning implies that we shouldn't expect to be able to routinely identify, recruit, select, and deploy leaders for every global position who are stars along all five dimensions. As discussed above, it is much more likely that our recruitment efforts will uncover candidates who, based on our interviews and observations, show strong tendencies along only a subset of the global behaviors. Given the dearth of highly qualified and experienced candidates, the practical thing to do is to go with them and arm them with information about the behaviors they should be working on. And then we need to do what we tend to do in any case—initially, if at all possible, send them to countries that are at least somewhat similar to their home bases. Possibly more important and more feasible, we need to send them before they're needed, before a crisis arises, and before any leaders being replaced leave and return home.

The third and final learning revolves around the role of culture in translating the behaviors of transglobal leaders into effectiveness. As noted earlier in this chapter, our previous research and experiences suggested that transglobal leaders become successful, at least in part, by creating and reinforcing a constructive culture within their organizations. Our work over the years with Leadership/Impact, which is frequently used for 360-degree feedback and executive development, has confirmed that leaders who accentuate positive and prescriptive strategies have a constructive impact on the people around them and their organization. *Prescriptive leaders* share with others their vision of the future and the goals to be attained, take supportive actions to guide and help people work toward that vision, and provide others with positive feedback and reinforcement when they are moving things in the right direction. More specifically, these leaders accentuate and create a setting that is oriented toward achievement, self-actualizing, humanistic-encouraging, and affiliative behaviors:

Achievement. They motivate and encourage others to set challenging but realistic goals, establish plans to meet those goals, and pursue them with enthusiasm. (Example: take reasonable risks to attain better results.)

Self-actualizing. They motivate and encourage others to gain enjoyment from their work, develop themselves professionally, and approach problems with interest, creativity, and integrity. (Example: think in unique and independent ways.)

Humanistic-encouraging. They motivate and encourage others to be supportive of people, help those around them to grow and develop, and provide others with positive feedback. (Example: train new people.)

Affiliative. They motivate and encourage others to treat people as members of the team, be sensitive to the needs of others, and interact in friendly and cooperative ways. (Example: emphasize the importance of the team.)

We originally discussed the possibility that leaders with high levels of the various facets of intelligence would encourage these constructive behaviors and create a positive culture. As we learned more about uncertainty resilience, team connectivity, and the other global dimensions, the potential impact of global behaviors on culture became even more apparent. For example, team connectivity sets the stage for affiliative behaviors, talent orientation for humanistic and encouraging styles, uncertainty resilience for the growth and innovation associated with self-actualizing behaviors, and pragmatic flexibility for results- and achievement-oriented behaviors. For purposes of illustration, these four cultural styles are positioned at the top of the "culture profile" in Figure 4.1—and we expected those to be the styles or cultural norms promoted by transglobal leaders. The length of the extensions along these styles (in the constructive styles segment on the profile) represents the expected strength of this constructive impact.

In contrast, it seemed that more local leaders would be less likely to have a constructive impact. Their behaviors instead were expected to have a more passive/defensive or possibly aggressive/defensive impact. A passive/defensive impact is associated with norms and expectations for approval, conventional, dependent, and avoidance behaviors:

> **Approval.** The leaders motivate and require others to gain the approval of those around them, to "go along" with people, and to maintain (superficially) pleasant interpersonal relationships. (Example: put forth only those ideas and suggestions that are likely to "please" others.)
>
> **Conventional.** The leaders motivate and require others to conform, fit into the "mold," and follow rules, policies, and

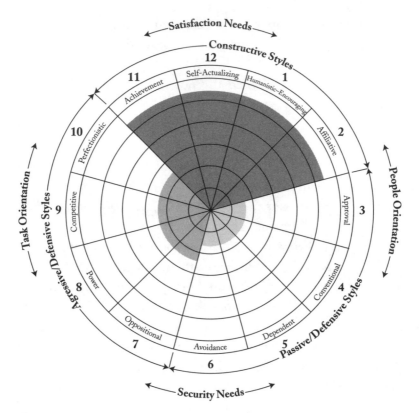

Figure 4.1 The Impact of Transglobal Leaders on Organizational Culture

Source: Profile and constructive style descriptions adapted from Leadership/ Impact inventory and feedback report with permission. Copyright 1996 by Human Synergistics International. All rights reserved.

standard operating procedures. (Example: refer to rules and procedures to justify actions.)

Dependent. The leaders motivate and require others to do only what they are told, clear all decisions with superiors, and please those in positions of authority. (Example: delay taking action until receiving clearances or approvals.)

Avoidance. The leaders motivate and require others to avoid any possibility of being blamed for a mistake, shift responsibilities to others, and maintain a low profile. (Example: take few chances.)

An aggressive/defensive impact is associated with norms and expectations for oppositional, power-oriented, competitive, and perfectionistic behaviors:

Oppositional. The leaders motivate and drive others to point out mistakes, gain status by being critical, and dismiss even good ideas due to minor flaws. (Example: are critical and hard to impress.)

Power. The leaders motivate and drive others to act forcefully and aggressively, control the people around them, and build up their power base. (Example: provide information to others on a need-to-know basis only.)

Competitive. The leaders motivate and drive others to operate in a win-lose framework, outperform their peers, and do anything necessary to look good. (Example: manipulate situations to enhance their own position.)

Perfectionistic. The leaders motivate and drive others to set unrealistically high goals, stay on top of every detail, and work long hours to attain narrowly defined objectives. (Example: give the impression they always have the answer or the necessary information.)

A more passive/defensive and aggressive/defensive impact is represented by the profile in Figure 4.2.

Our survey results show that the five global dimensions turn out to impact people and be related to organization culture in the ways suggested by these profiles. That is, many of the survey items measuring team connectivity, uncertainty resilience, and the other dimensions are positively related to a constructive impact. It is

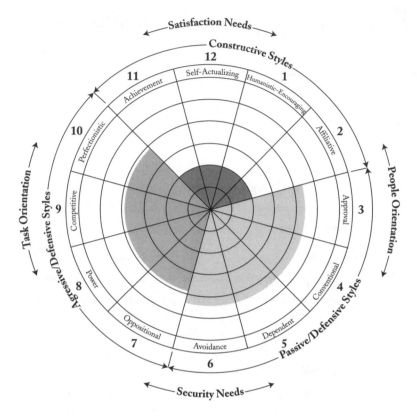

Figure 4.2 The Impact of Local Leaders on Organizational Culture

Source: Profile and constructive style descriptions adapted from Leadership/ Impact inventory and feedback report with permission. Copyright 1996 by Human Synergistics International. All rights reserved.

noted that this is not always the case with pragmatic flexibility, given that a couple of these items appear to operate in a reverse manner. Overall, however, the global behaviors not only have a constructive impact but also tend to be associated with a weak passive/defensive impact. Finally, the correlations between the global dimensions and the aggressive/defensive styles were weak and not significant.

This connection between the global dimensions and impact is important given that various studies based on the Leadership/

Impact Survey have shown that leaders with a constructive impact are more effective than those with a defensive impact. Furthermore, studies based on the Human Synergistics Organizational Culture Inventory (which more broadly measures the cultural norms and expectations prevailing in organizations) have shown that the constructive styles lead to organizational effectiveness and sustainability whereas the passive/defensive styles detract from these outcomes.

Just as important, international research and consulting with the Organizational Culture Inventory has shown that the constructive styles are viewed as ideal and appropriate by members of organizations located in practically every country in the world. In contrast, the defensive styles, particularly the passive/defensive styles, are less consistently accepted and endorsed. While they are viewed as acceptable in certain countries (for example, some South American and Southeast Asian countries), they are fairly strongly rejected in other countries (for example, Anglo and European countries). This suggests that transglobal leaders create and sustain organizational cultures that are almost universally accepted. On the other hand, local leaders are more likely to create cultures that are rejected and viewed as counterproductive by at least some members of their international teams.

Thus, the final thing we learned is that the behaviors exhibited by transglobal leaders promote effectiveness not only directly but also indirectly via the impact of those behaviors on members and the cultures of their organizations. Transglobal leaders create an organization culture that people from diverse societal backgrounds view as appropriate, that stimulates behaviors that promote teamwork and a results orientation, and that de-emphasizes norms for behaviors that get in the way of doing business globally. This learning leads us to replace our original model of transglobal leadership with the revised and expanded framework shown in Figure 4.3.

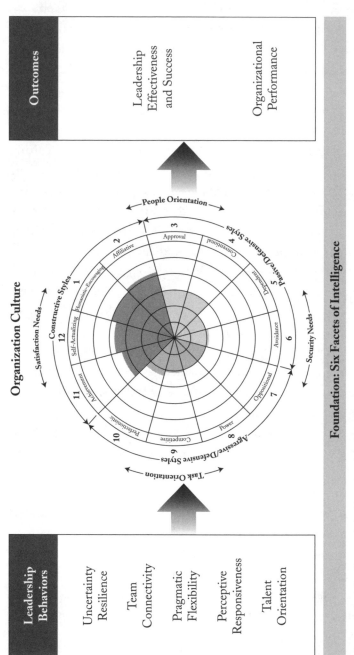

Figure 4.3 The Transglobal Leadership Model

CONCLUSION

Through this research and the use of the above model we were able to segue from our original notion of the "Quantum Leader" to what we are now calling the "Transglobal Leader." This is the leader who takes the notions of transformational leadership to the next level and embodies the five behavioral dimensions in the context of the globe.

As a result of our analysis and interviews we discovered significant differences between our transglobal leaders and those who are better suited for more local leadership roles. We have captured these differences in our Transglobal versus Local Leader Chart (Table 5.1). We also developed a Transglobal Leadership Matrix (Table 5.2)—a matrix that defines how these five behavioral dimensions play out in the business world so you can recognize them. Both the chart and matrix are discussed in detail in the next part of the book. If we have piqued your interest, please read on for more insight and cases to see these leaders in action!

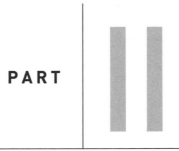

THE NUTS AND BOLTS OF TRANSGLOBAL LEADERS: WHAT THEY DO, HOW THEY THINK, AND HOW THEY INTERACT WITH OTHERS TO BUILD SUSTAINABLE BUSINESSES

Part II of this book is designed to give you a complete picture of what it takes to be a transglobal leader. This part goes into detail about the new realm of diversity in which all of us will be immersed as globalization becomes more and more prevalent.

Chapter 5 examines the differences between transglobal leaders and local leaders. We draw a sharp distinction between great local leaders and great transglobal leaders. The dimensions of transglobal leaders' behaviors are fully discussed, including how to spot people who have this potential. The Transglobal Leadership Matrix at a Glance in Table 5.2 summarizes the five essential characteristics (behaviors) discussed in this chapter.

Chapter 6 takes diversity and globalization to the next level. This chapter will help you see how the diversity dialog is changing now and how it will continue to change in the future as more businesses increase their globalization efforts. We lay out a compelling process for embracing the global diversity that is in your organization now and that will be increasing in the future. The Transglobal Leadership Diversity Matrix in Table 6.2 spells out what transglobal leaders do to ensure that globally diverse teams can offer powerful performance in their organizations. And, as in other chapters, case studies are provided to highlight how effective transglobal leaders have made diversity work for their organizations.

CHAPTER 5

The Behavioral Dimensions of Transglobal Leaders: What Sets Them Apart?

A ship in a harbor is safe, but that's not what ships are built for.
—WILLIAM SHEDD,
NINETEENTH-CENTURY THEOLOGIAN

As we went through the Transglobal Leadership Matrix and the original survey questions we constructed relative to the intelligences discussed in Part I, we found clear contrasts. And when we analyzed our leaders' survey results, we saw that there were real differences between the best transglobal leaders and those who function better in more local settings. We also saw numerous commonalities between the great leaders across our data sets. Possibly most important, both sets of great leaders have a constructive impact on the culture of their organizations.

What is not surprising is that good leadership has some universal characteristics. But there are also very clear distinctions as well. What we will explore here are the commonalities—what they both do well, as there are great leaders in both arenas—and which of these characteristics are key dimensions of transglobal leaders. This chapter's primary purpose is to give you deep insight into transglobal leaders: who they are, how to distinguish them from other leaders, and what is it that they do every day that sets them apart. When you are finished with this chapter, you should be able to look around your organization and have a good sense of which individuals have transglobal leadership potential, whether they are currently in a global role or not.

TRANSGLOBAL VERSUS LOCAL LEADERS

The literature is replete with what it takes to be a great leader, so we will not regurgitate this. However, we will sum up the essential commonalities we know great local and transglobal leaders must have—because certain qualities contribute to great leadership no matter where you are.

Great leaders in our sample (both local and global) all possess, at least to some degree, the following traits:

- Strategic orientation
- Vision

- Client focus

- Good people leadership skills

- Results orientation

- Team focus

- Strong moral compass and high integrity

- Adaptability

The differences, however, are quite telling. Table 5.1 lays out the significant areas of contrast so that you can clearly see the differences. While the contrast in some cases is relatively black and white, this comparison does highlight the significant differences and subtleties that distinguish the two types of leaders.

Some overwhelmingly significant differences are due to the complexity and ambiguity of the environments in which the transglobal leaders function. For instance, transglobal leaders don't have to work hard at inclusion and diversity, for they are unconsciously competent in this area. It is in their evolved DNA. They don't have to be convinced to try new things; they do it naturally. Adventure is second nature to them, and they are always looking for the new next best thing. They have developed themselves to become natural innovators. Local leaders, in contrast, often can be more conforming. They can also be innovators, but the realm of innovation is in a narrower sphere. Transglobal leaders take their ideas and adapt them to new and vastly broader and more complex environments. Transglobal leaders are much more likely to support and help shape unique approaches to work, while local leaders are wonderful at stable operations and building like-minded teams who will deliver goals in a repeatable and reliable manner. At times they may be suspicious of new ways of doing things and can hold on to current practices until it is too late to make a change or the market opportunity has passed. Just as in all things, the positive transglobal leadership attributes just described can be used to excess, in which

Table 5.1 Transglobal Versus Local Leaders

Transglobal Leaders	Local Leaders
Uncertainty Resilience	
1. Respond effectively to subtle, seemingly unclear, expressions of disagreement. 2. Create and nurture teams that are as talented and diverse as possible. 3. Constantly seek out team members with different perspectives who challenge norms and assumptions. 4. Accentuate the potential benefits of innovations to the organization. 5. Take on projects and assignments that are new and different.	1. Collaborate with, confide in, and develop people similar to them. 2. Create teams and develop members who reflect their own background and perspective. 3. Respond best to situations that are structured, relatively certain, and predictable. 4. Work best with others in familiar situations. 5. Take things literally.
Team Connectivity	
1. Redefine personal work activities in consideration of the work needs of others. 2. Communicate effectively by listening to others. 3. Attain goals by working with and supporting colleagues. 4. See and interpret problems, events, and situations through the eyes of others.	1. Expect others to redefine their roles to support own role, work needs, and expectations. 2. Respect others' autonomy and expect them to be self-sufficient. 3. Refer to problems, external factors, and other people when explaining mistakes and performance problems. 4. Tend to emphasize own individual contributions more than team successes.
Pragmatic Flexibility	
1. Seem comfortable adjusting style when negotiating with others. 2. Challenge personal biases and beliefs to constantly stretch and broaden perspective. 3. Balance the need for achieving global consistency and adjusting to local norms. 4. Modify rules and procedures when they interfere with implementing and completing tasks.	1. Refuse to deal with organizational politics. 2. Appreciate diversity but are grounded and comfortable seeing things from own perspective. 3. Emphasize global consistency over local adaptation. 4. Emphasize structure, formal policies, and standard operating procedures.

(continued on next page)

Table 5.1 Transglobal Versus Local Leaders *(continued)*

Perceptive Responsiveness	
1. Emphasize the individuality of clients and other stakeholders. 2. Focus on intangible rewards and tailor rewards to the individual—one size does not fit all. 3. Make decisions as if the customer base could change in the future. 4. Forgive cultural foibles and can deal with unique interpersonal challenges. 5. Connect with others by mirroring their behaviors and adjusting style.	1. Treat everyone the same in the name of fairness. 2. Focus heavily on compensation as the principal reward mechanism; are comfortable with one-size-fits-all approaches. 3. Make decisions as if tomorrow's customers will be the same as today's. 4. Assume local concerns can adjust to corporate policies and practices. 5. Treat experience-based assumptions as facts that shouldn't be challenged.
Talent Orientation	
1. Personally involved in, and take responsibility for, people development. 2. Tap human potential to drive results; emphasize employee engagement. 3. Help people grow by providing feedback and encouragement. 4. Talk about the importance of people to the organization.	1. Though willing to help, view human resources department as responsible for development of talent. 2. At times, focus primarily on the bottom line. 3. Emphasize technical and structural change over people achieving change. 4. Emphasize recruitment over development as a means for strengthening the organization.
Other	
1. Take personal responsibility for community involvement and sustainability. 2. Try to learn and make an effort to speak and read local languages. 3. More universalistic—make an effort to travel, learn, and experience new things. 4. Emphasize CI, EI, and GI as key drivers for achieving excellence.	1. Expect government to take the lead with the community and create community sustainability. 2. Assume that others will adjust to their language needs and limitations. 3. More paternalistic—stay close to the safe and familiar comfort zone. 4. Emphasize IQ, BI, and MI as key drivers for attaining performance.

case they can have the opposite effect on their organization's performance and the leaders' followers.

The good news is that the behavioral dimensions of transglobal leaders can be developed over time. The leaders we studied constantly worked at perfecting their leadership. They focused on it and were open to new and challenging experiences. Mark Hutchinson recalls, "When I got to China, I had so much to learn! I am constantly learning and being challenged to think differently. It's exciting and exhilarating but also a bit daunting." Hutchinson typifies the behavior we see in the transglobal leaders—the thirst for learning and stretching one's leadership capability.

We do not want to imply that transglobal leaders are "good" and local leaders are "bad": organizations need both depending on where their focus lies and what their strategy is. The mix can clearly depend on what organizations need to achieve over the next three to five years. There are great leaders in both camps and some in between. But one thing is certain: you will not be successful at driving strong results and growing the business if you are a global company with a substantial number of leaders with a local versus global mindset.

We are reminded of the widely publicized experience of Facebook as it tried to do business in China with a local mindset. Facebook naïvely assumed that everyone valued open space communication as much as it did. Few would dispute that freedom of speech is a valued element of life. Facebook was trying to drive a value that many in the world would say was laudable, but its approach to doing so was perhaps wrong. While it may be true that the Chinese citizenry might have wanted great open space communication, the government clearly did not, and Facebook was resoundingly resisted in that market by the Chinese government. A different approach based on a greater understanding of the political and societal differences might have allowed Facebook to ultimately pursue its open communication value for the longer haul. But now the Chinese government will be suspicious of any efforts Facebook takes to enter the Chinese market.

Simply put, what we are talking about is getting the right mix of leadership talent to keep the company sustainable and profitable over time both locally and globally. Now let's take a deeper dive into what our research told us are the five behaviors that underpin the mindsets and approaches of successful transglobal leaders.

THE FIVE BEHAVIORAL DIMENSIONS OF TRANSGLOBAL LEADERS AND HOW THEY PLAY OUT IN THE WORKPLACE

As we completed our research, we cut through all the noise about global leadership and were able to boil the essential elements down to five critical behavioral dimensions. While transglobal leaders have skills and characteristics beyond these, without these five, they may not be as successful as they could be in achieving high performance in the context of large transglobal leadership roles. Let's review the five behavioral dimensions briefly before we go into greater detail about them in this chapter:

> **Uncertainty resilience.** Building on differences and complexity. Able to function in ambiguous and vague environments.

> **Team connectivity.** Working across boundaries and borders. Able to integrate and connect activities and ideas from wherever they are conceived.

> **Pragmatic flexibility.** Adapting to other cultures both from the organization and the country culture perspectives. Able to flex their value sets to adjust to other mores and norms.

> **Perceptive responsiveness.** Operating with a high degree of sensitivity to others' needs. Able to function through intuition as well as facts.

Talent orientation. Focusing on the development of people as a key lever for success. Able and willing to personally take responsibility for talent development.

Time and time again we saw these dimensions play out in the leaders we observed. In this section, we define each dimension and provide the contexts in which it shows itself so that you can recognize it. We will be sharing examples and stories from the leaders we studied to further illuminate each dimension. Specifically, we will be looking at each dimension through the following lenses:

- Characteristic and uncharacteristic behaviors
- The leaders' orientation, for example, toward change or the status quo
- What they typically emphasize when talking
- What they respond negatively to
- What they are unlikely to do
- Their impact on organizational culture
- How they are viewed by others both positively and negatively
- Their leadership strengths

By reviewing the dimensions in this context, you will have a clear picture of how transglobal leaders operate in a global world and business context.

UNCERTAINTY RESILIENCE: BUILDING ON DIFFERENCES AND COMPLEXITY

Much has been written about the ability to deal with ambiguity and how critical this is as companies become more complex. As Meg

Wheatley said in her seminal book *Dealing with Chaos*, leaders of the future will need to be able to tolerate chaos and make sense out of it for those they lead. She further pointed out that problems and solutions could often be vague and that leaders will have to weed through lots of information to make sense of situations.[1]

This ability to make sense of circumstances that are chaotic, unclear, complicated, or vague becomes even more important in the global context. Not only can the elements of a situation be confusing and unclear but also the context of the situation can be unfamiliar, making it difficult for leaders to fall back on tried-and-true past approaches or methods. Mores, customs, and approaches to work and thinking styles all come into play in the global arena. We found that the leaders who are most successful in this environment are able to deal with ambiguity, and they also have a high degree of tolerance for it. Simply put, these leaders can see patterns and make sense out of unclear situations and can take action in the face of not having all the information. In fact, these leaders reported they are extremely comfortable in such situations and help followers feel comfortable so that they are not paralyzed by confusion or ambiguity. In situations in which they do not understand what is going on, they are very comfortable in revealing this to their team.

Characteristically, these leaders can read the environment from multiple vantage points. They are able to look through many lenses to interpret the situation and can see things through many points of view, such as that of the local market, the customers, or the government. They interpret these points from a figurative orientation and can create a broad vision and direction to deal with the situation. Mark Hutchinson, head of GE China, put it this way: "I spend time listening to customers, getting to know them, talking to numerous people in a new market. I hang out with my staff and really try to understand what they see as the issues and the nuances of the situation. I also ask a lot of questions because I know that's how people communicate and what they say can be interpreted differently. I don't want to lay my interpretation over what I think I have heard. Then I take all this information, and with my team I sift through it to make sense and find the right relative way forward. This attribute helped me to avoid a very costly mistake as I was entering a new market. We took the right direction and succeeded on all fronts." Hutchinson also noted that he didn't want to make assumptions about what others believe. He wanted to find out what they actually believe. He thought, for example, that China didn't want multinationals, but that was not the case. He had to really listen to learn this truth.

All the transglobal leaders we studied do the same thing. They make it a point to "seek first to understand" and then create a framework for action. They do not need to have detailed operational plans; rather, they operate from frameworks that provide for overarching direction that allows for local adaptation.

The flip side of this, however, is that they often have an aversion to overanalyzing innovation from a cost and risk point of view. They do not need continuity and stability in their work environment, and these elements are not important for them to be successful. In fact, they tend to be bored with situations that have too much stability, and they often seek change or new challenges when the dynamics of the situation become stable. These leaders are excited by innovation and change, and they are excited, if not exhilarated, by situations that require new thinking, innovative approaches, and uncharted paths. They are clearly oriented to change, and complexity does not frighten them; on the contrary, change and complexity challenge them and keep them excited. They enjoy trying to make sense of things.

These leaders are visionaries who see opportunities in the face of adversity and can help others see these opportunities as well. They have a high tolerance for ambiguity and are constantly communicating their vision to others. They create calm yet a sense of excitement, and focus through vision and frameworks. They try to balance local customization with global consistency.

UNCERTAINTY RESILIENCE IN ACTION

When discussing how important it is to be able to handle ambiguity and sometimes just not knowing the situation at all, Steve Sargent, president and CEO of GE Australia and New Zealand, shared an important story which we're summarizing here.

As an organization, GE saw the importance of this ability during the global financial crisis as some leaders thrived and others struggled. During this terrible period, leaders needed to find clarity out of confusion. The successful ones shared two characteristics:

- **Confidence.** They displayed confidence even when they did not have all the answers. For them, it was about handling ambiguity and dealing effectively with events none of them had experienced before.

- **Excellent communication practices.** They were able to communicate clearly and candidly with their teams.

The successful leaders were comfortable in saying to their teams that they didn't know where and how the situation was going to end and, though they knew where they were today, they didn't know what was coming.

Those who did well had to be ambidextrous and almost schizophrenic; this period required integrated and exceptionally clear thinking. They had to anticipate a number of different occurrences on the horizon and be able to translate them down to the business level. They then had to internalize the events and put them into context for their team so the team members could understand things in their own terms. Those leaders who did not do as well got caught up in the confusion, didn't understand what their own responses should be, and as a result stopped communicating.

In certain ways, Steve's observations of leaders dealing successfully with crises run parallel to those of Ranjay Gulati, a business professor at both Kellogg and Harvard Business School, who has been studying successful leaders and companies that operate globally: "If you are in a remote area where you are the representative of the headquarters in a local context, you have to operate as a bilingual translator. You need to communicate what the head office is trying to do, what their goals are and why, and you need to do it as clearly as possible. At the same time you have to raise the sensibility of headquarters to the local context."

TEAM CONNECTIVITY: INTEGRATING ACROSS BOUNDARIES

The term *team connectivity* refers to a leader's ability to create and work with teams across borders and boundaries and connect the work of all teams in powerful ways to help transfer knowledge and capture great ideas from across the globe that can be adapted to particular settings. Team connectivity is different from intact team development because it means connecting teams across country boundaries and often across organizational systems.

Transglobal leaders enable dialogue. They bring people together so they can collaborate. They create open communication across the organization where learning is valued and shared no matter where it comes from. These leaders do not necessarily view teams as those they directly influence. Their natural bent is to form teams and networks of people around projects that are focused on innovation or customer needs. They are comfortable working with virtual teams, and they can provide the leadership and focus for these teams to function well in a virtual world.

These leaders approach their role much more from a visionary point of view to help set future directions and goals and then step back and facilitate the team's interaction rather than direct it. As Peter Block described in his work on leadership, they become the "steward" of the team.[2] In the global world, stewardship of people will take on a whole new dimension and level of importance. The transglobal leaders' roles can be equated with those of neurons and synapses. They help connect thinking around the globe to spark ideas and innovation that lead to the creation of great new products and enhanced services. They are blind to seniority level, generation, and location and to their own need for power and control. They are focused, sparking ideas through connectivity and bringing the best thinking and ideas of others into action.

John Forrest, head of corporate solutions at Jones Lang LaSalle, illustrates the need for connectivity this way: "I have to operate on a local and a global stage every day. Overseeing the real estate needs of global companies like Panasonic, Microsoft, Infosys, and Procter & Gamble, truly global companies, is constantly confronting. These companies demand global service continuity but each has local idiosyncrasies that also need to be serviced. It's only through accessing and allowing active participation from our local on-the-ground teams that we can build an operating mechanism that works for us and our clients. Without the connection and dialog between local, regional, and global teams, we are unlikely to meet the client's full breadth of needs."

These leaders are not just pie-in-the-sky visionaries who support unrealistic goals or strategies or let their teams loose to develop outlandish proposals. Rather, they are personally involved and grounded. They are not constrained by, but rather they embrace, thinking that is different from their own. They help shape the team, guide direction, challenge thinking, and support implementation so that the team can achieve sustainable results. They are acutely aware of their own accountability for team action and provide "air cover" for the work of the team so that the team can be successful. If the team fails or falters, these leaders do not cast blame but rather look at what could have been done differently, and they take personal responsibility for helping the team learn and ultimately become successful. To sum it up, these leaders adjust their activities to the needs of the team and enable the team to be successful.

Transglobal leaders are truly able to subjugate their biases to see issues, problems, and possibilities from many perspectives. It is highly uncharacteristic of these leaders to expect others to see the world from their point of view. This does not mean that they don't have a point of view, rather it is shaped by many experiences, conversations, and exposure to extensive perspectives so that they challenge themselves and their thinking to ensure that it is not colored by their local bias. This is not to say that transglobal leaders are chameleons with no perspective of their own and that they go with the flow of the group—they do not. Rather, they create effective and overarching global teams for their companies and help connect the best minds in defining, refining, and developing powerful solutions for success. These leaders are truly global citizens in search of the best solutions that support the greater good.

They reject power orientations and individualistic approaches. They do not function on the basis of personal greed or personal motivation, but rather, they work toward the best approach for the most people—the employees, the company, customers, and the community. We'd rather not recount here the numerous examples of leaders who have deliberately or inadvertently brought harm to a company, its employees, the environment, customers, or the community; the press is replete with accounts of such stories and there are numerous books written about personal and corporate greed. We can say, however, that you will be hard-pressed to find a true transglobal leader in these stories. You will rarely see a transglobal leader act selfishly or at another's expense.

We have read enough 360-degree feedback reports, employee surveys, and cultural analyses to know that there are still plenty of leaders in corporations today who think first about "What's in it for me?" and then act to ensure self-preservation. You can probably cite numerous examples from your own experience of egotistical, self-centered leaders whose decisions are driven by the desire to first make themselves look good instead of achieving something for the greater good of the team or the organization. Transglobal leaders embody behavior, language, and actions that clearly and consistently demonstrate that they value collaboration, support, and "What's in it for the team?" as opposed to themselves.

Most of the transglobal leaders we interviewed cited stories about what they did when confronted with greed, egotism, or personal self-interest. In all cases, they sought roles elsewhere rather than conform to this type of philosophy. As the CEO of GE China, Mark Hutchinson demonstrated this point very well early in his career before joining GE. He was asked to participate in acts that were clearly in the personal self-interest of a small group of people. He knew he would be rewarded handsomely if he conformed. He did not, and he left the company of his own accord. Several years later, the team was disbanded and the unit leaders left in disgrace.

When you scratch the surface of great transglobal leaders, you will see that they are constantly seeking personal mastery. They are highly reflective and keenly aware of their own strengths and what they continually need to develop on a personal front. However, such leaders are in danger of four misperceptions by others and can be erroneously viewed as:

- Being overly accommodating to the views of the team and losing sight of the overall driving purpose for which the team was created.

- Too altruistic.

- "Avatars," so closely aligning themselves with a new culture in which they are residing that they lose objectivity for what's good for the overall organization.

- Being such a complete opposite of the "company man" that they have rendered themselves ineffective on all fronts. They are incorrectly perceived as constantly challenging the system that they are supposed to represent.

To sum up, nevertheless, transglobal leaders who create team connectivity are broad leaders who, in the words of Peter Schwartz, "take the long view" and mobilize their people around this vision to achieve remarkable results.[3] They create constructive cultures in which organization members feel a strong sense of achievement and personal accomplishment in working with them. As a result, they typically have higher degrees of employee satisfaction and engagement, and in turn, they experience less employee turnover. Such leaders are talent magnets: people, regardless of gender, age, or nationality, want to work for them. Our data analyses showed that effective transglobal leaders have a strong positive impact on their followers and create highly humanistic cultures that, in turn, support high performance. Our transglobal leaders have achieved great organizational success and are still achieving outstanding results in extremely complex, diverse, and at times highly ambiguous environments.

TEAM CONNECTIVITY IN ACTION

Maarten Kelder, managing partner of Monitor Group in Asia, is surrounded by diversity. "In my industry we thrive on diversity, we see it in our teams and our clients. What makes it more complex in Asia is that we deal with so many cultures and nationalities. In my team alone I have over 20 nationalities. In a typical project meeting, we will have six to seven cultures represented. But I believe this is what helps us create better outcomes. Sure, it is harder to make a decision, and it takes longer to get alignment, but ultimately the decisions you make are better when coming out of different perspectives."

To Steve Sargent, president and CEO of GE Australia and New Zealand, the development of leaders is far more important today. "You know what made me a successful leader 10 years ago won't make me a successful leader 5 years from now. Because the world is changing dramatically. In technology, 10 or 15 years ago the people at the top had all the knowledge. . . . If as an organization you think you have the knowledge at the top, you are completely upside down. We used to operate through a defined matrix where I hard lined reported to you and dotted lined to her. Or I functionally reported to you or operationally reported to him. That was a concept developed by McKenzie in 1957. In a large company now with multi products and many countries, that just does not work. Everyone today, not just leaders, needs to work in interconnected and interdependent networks. That's how we work today. You need to know how to communicate within those networks, how to leverage them, and to do this successfully, you need a high degree of awareness and flexibility. It gets back to being able to handle ambiguity. It's no longer simple enough to make decisions based on hierarchy because frankly the hierarchy does not exist in this system. It's not even just a dual matrix anymore because you have function; you've got a region; you've got customer groups; and you may have up to four or five different lenses with which to view pretty much everything you do. It's a much more complex world to live in and manage within. You need to be well connected and attuned on multiple levels."

Rob Salmon, executive vice president of field operations for NetApp, is passionate about team connectivity. He defines it as "moving away from the hierarchy to interconnect molecules of people working together from diverse parts of the company to allow the creativity to flow. These pods of people from all parts of NetApp feel unleashed to come up with new and exciting ideas for growth. Using John Kotter and his ideas from *Leading Change*, we started a small pilot of interconnected teams and helped shape the teams to be diverse and to focus on innovation, which started to go viral. It's been so successful that when the team's work is done, they go back to their work location and take what they have learned through the process and start their own molecules of creativity and teach others how to do it. It's all about letting go and not having to drive innovative change but rather, allowing it to flourish."

Pragmatic Flexibility: Adapting to Cultures

Typically, one of the most significant challenges faced by authors, scholars, and pundits when writing yet another book on leadership is to come up with new and trendy terms for ideas that have been written about before. There have been so many books churned out on leadership that there is relatively little new under the sun. We ran into somewhat the opposite situation and a different set of challenges in working on the Transglobal Leadership Survey; that is, we came up with a finding that was so different and unexpected that we really weren't sure what to do with it.

So we improvised and talked about it during numerous conference calls, reran the data, and reviewed the results a few times, and we obsessed over positive and negative correlations to make sure we weren't interpreting things backward. We then tried to understand how and why a behavior that might be interpreted negatively could actually be considered rather enlightened, helping to bring together people with diverse values and standards, and enhancing organizational effectiveness. After dedicating sufficient time and attention to these scholarly tasks, we went back to work and took on the more typical challenge of coming up with a trendy name for the behavior.

In meeting this challenge, we converged on the term *pragmatic flexibility*. In behavioral terms, pragmatic flexibility involves bending rules and regulations as required by the situation, adjusting personal values to get the job done, and relying on unwritten norms and the informal work group to make things happen. This flexibility also involves showing compassion, even if it jeopardizes the task at hand, as opposed to focusing on task accomplishment in a detached manner. It's not that transglobal leaders engage in these behaviors all the time; they just do so slightly more often than leaders who are viewed as more suitable for local assignments. These behaviors sometimes can come at the cost of strategies and behaviors that seem upright and solid—including refusing to compromise on principles, maintaining personal integrity at all costs, and paying attention to rules and "how things are supposed to work." As such, these behaviors are exhibited only occasionally and judiciously.

In demonstrating these behaviors, it is unlikely that transglobal leaders are compromising on clear-cut ethical issues such as bribery. However, when they run into conflicts and problems around such issues, they may show more sensitivity than local leaders to the reality that the conflicts are the result of differences in societal values and practices, differences across countries in the maturity of management as a discipline and profession, and differences in experiences and role models. They may also be less likely to emphatically label certain practices "unethical" and instead spend time on disentangling behaviors that constitute true self-serving ethical breaches versus those that are driven by norms to show respect, deference, or appreciation. Their measured responses to inappropriate practices and their efforts to identify superordinate solutions to ethical dilemmas appear to create a less defensive and more transparent culture than the more dogmatic alternative. Within a diverse and global context, the discussions that they encourage around ethics can lead to a greater sensitivity on the part of diverse members to ensure they act appropriately from a cross-cultural perspective.

Transglobal leaders, therefore, are distinguished by a propensity toward openness; because they are rarely dogmatic, others view them as willing to listen even if they feel strongly about an issue. While they are committed to the organization, they dislike bureaucracy, gather information through informal networks, understand the power of unwritten rules, and won't let established systems and structures get in the way of goal attainment. In that respect, they are strongly goal and achievement oriented, but at the same time, they realize that the best way to get things done is through people. This, in turn, leads them to spend time with their groups (both peers and subordinates) on gaining consensus and commitment.

In working with diverse groups, pragmatic flexibility requires and implies carefully honed negotiation skills. The transglobal leader talks about "possibilities" and develops higher-order solutions that not only transcend differences in values but also add value for all concerned. However, when superordinate solutions cannot be identified, transglobal leaders are perfectly willing to compromise in order to move things forward and get issues of low importance out of the way. Trade-offs and give-and-take are relied on when necessary and appropriate.

Leaders who are pragmatically flexible respond negatively to power-oriented and conventional thinking. They dislike working within organizations that are hierarchically structured or those that saddle members with rules, regulations, and traditions. Similarly, they dislike working with people who are authoritarian and conservative. While they generally are quite accepting of people who differ from themselves, they have a somewhat difficult time with those who truly value power distance and expect others to conform to their ways of thinking. Transglobal leaders are unlikely to be unyielding or dismissive of others' viewpoints, and they prefer not to work with those who behave in these ways.

Pragmatic flexibility translates into the ability to adjust to different approaches, perspectives, and situational demands in a global context. Leaders with this ability come across as tolerant and understanding, and, in the best of circumstances, they are viewed as skilled negotiators and consensus builders. If taken too far, though, flexible leaders may be seen as vacillating and malleable and, under the worst of circumstances, instrumental or even unprincipled. Under most circumstances, however, this flexibility is viewed as a plus for transglobal leadership and creates an organizational setting that suppresses these potentially negative tendencies.

PRAGMATIC FLEXIBILITY IN ACTION

Richard Solomons, an Englishman, prior to becoming global CEO for the InterContinental Hotels Group (IHG), had to take over, on short notice, as the U.S. president of IHG after the sudden death of the incumbent, Steve Porter. Solomons had learned during two previous stints in the United States that Americans have a high emotional engagement with leadership, far more than he had experienced elsewhere. "Steve Porter was a very highly respected and loved leader. Among other things, we knew we had to quickly set up a website to enable staff to express their emotions; it was staggering the number of people who had emotional outpourings and the depth of those feelings. It was very touching. It would never have happened in the United Kingdom, Europe, or Australia. It became very obvious that we needed to honor him and his legacy, and a range of things were done including setting up an education fund. And this had to be dealt with quickly; it was just the right thing to do."

Gary Budzinski, formerly a senior executive at HP and an American, took over a global team of 40,000 employees at HP. The first step he took was to understand the values and cultural nuances of the countries in his scope. He personally visited every country, but he also took another powerful step. He launched a cultural diagnosis of all the countries and talked about the differences and similarities of each with the teams. "This created great transparency about the values that we all thought were important for us to embrace. If I had just come in with my values without understanding the nuances and flexing to them, I would have been dead on arrival as the new leader. This ability to create transparency and engage the teams in discussion of the important values for us going forward was essential."

Margaret Keane, CEO and president of GE Capital Retail Finance, spends considerable time understanding the values and cultural norms of the global teams in her organization. She takes the time to listen to what is important to them and how best to support them in their roles servicing clients and customers. As she has put it, "I have to listen and understand what's important to both parties. By understanding local customs and values, we help the teams translate the customer requirements and needs so the teams can be customer focused and successful. I can't do this from my office. I have to do this by going to our global locations, spending time with the employees to understand what makes them passionate about their roles and how best that connects to our customers' and clients' needs."

In practice, most of the situations requiring pragmatic flexibility do not involve ethical dilemmas or challenges. Many revolve around business or social customs and simply require graciousness and a readiness to make adjustments in one's behavior or decisions. This involves doing things that one might not otherwise do in their home setting.

Perceptive Responsiveness: Acting on Intuition and Fact

Transglobal leaders naturally and organically develop and display a global, cross-cultural mindset, maintaining openness to the changing needs of their employees and clients. Respect for cultural and behavioral differences and attention to the likes, dislikes, pet peeves, and pleasures of a diverse group are at the core and center of their personalities. Transglobal leaders pay very close attention to individuals in their audience, and they can detect subtle nuances in people's behaviors. This in turn influences their responses, thereby strengthening the bond between them and their stakeholders.

What we have identified as "perceptive responsiveness" in a leader can be learned and enhanced, even more so than some of the other behavioral dimensions. In our discussions with transglobal leaders, we found that they tend to very quickly immerse themselves in local cultural agendas and the mores and customs of the countries they work and live in or travel through. These leaders adapt well to any environment, and they are passionate about learning and discovery. They rely on factual evidence that informs their own personal style and behaviors toward individuals with whom they come in contact. One of the leaders we interviewed claimed that she makes explicit attempts to blend in and feel at home when in a new country or when dealing with diverse groups for the first time. When in a new setting, she gathers as much information as possible about her surroundings and its people, without seeming too intrusive. She reaches out to a few locals and asks them to help her get acclimated to her new surroundings. Her priority is not to join the local "American Club" and connect with her compatriots but to invest time and energy in activities and interactions that better help her understand her new environment and the people with whom she works.

The transglobal leaders we studied are vigilant and perceptive in terms of both their own emotions and those of others, using intuition and insight to achieve balance and harmony. While the local leaders might motivate through charisma and inspiration, using core values and principles, transglobal leaders extend beyond charisma and take a selfless, true-life approach, assessing each situation before acting and inspiring.

Successful transglobal leaders are very unlikely to take a one-size-fits-all approach; rather, they adapt well to cultural and situational variations. They conscientiously seek out and study individual characteristics and relish differences based on cultural norms, artifacts, values, and other factors. They recognize unique characteristics in individuals and are able to inspire performance through their sensitivity and inclusive style. They do not apply standardized rewards and recognition but instead base these on an appreciation of individual differences.

Our survey repeatedly demonstrated the value these leaders place on diversity and cultural differences and the innate impulse they have to make individuals feel welcome and comfortable, allowing them to excel in their own way rather than coercing them to a less natural and contrived level of performance. Many of the leaders we surveyed appeared quite content in a diverse setting, and they used both fact and intuition to simultaneously drive the comfort, credibility, and loyalty of their people.

Transglobal leaders are not daunted by change, and they can often anticipate the shifting and evolving needs of their customers long before these are articulated and expressed. They respond constructively to negative feedback, using this information to drive transformation or development. They are constantly scouting for new information so they can remain ahead of the curve, and they are often at the forefront of innovation. But most importantly they are acutely sensitive to the different preferences of the clients and the employees.

Transglobal leaders, however, run the risk of sometimes appearing unfair and inconsistent. Their craving for knowledge and learning and their perceptive responsiveness cause them to pay greater attention to unfamiliar details in certain individuals and to new and unknown protocols and norms, which can give the impression to others that they are giving preferential or partial treatment toward an individual or group. Similarly, their desire to reward people in individualized ways can be misinterpreted as favoritism.

PERCEPTIVE RESPONSIVENESS IN ACTION

For Steve Sargent, president and CEO of GE Australia and New Zealand, intuition is based on experience. "To be good at it," Sargent told us, "you need an above average level of intelligence and a good degree of experience, and you have to know the people on your team. Intuition becomes a more important asset as you move up in an organization. Earlier on, you will get ahead because you are the content expert. Then you start to get assigned to roles where you are no longer the content expert. This is when you need to know when and how to probe to understand people, when to discipline, when to fly high, and when to power back. To do that well takes experience, coaching, role modeling, and knowing when to reach out. Knowing you don't have all the answers or that your team may not have all the answers but having the experience and confidence to reach out to others for help and advice are key."

Clayton Daley, retired chairman and CFO of Procter & Gamble, when discussing intuition, noted, "Finance and accounting responsibilities, whether it's tax compliance, internal control, or audit, do not lend themselves on one level to a lot of intuition. Where intuition was important was at the leadership level—where it was *very* important. Where people could walk into a situation and understand what was not being said: What's going on here? What is it that people don't think they can talk about? You have to have a smell, and you have to deal with that smell. That's intuition for me, and in finance it was very necessary for the leadership team and senior people, if we were to continue to be successful."

Ranjay Gulati's book *Reorganize for Resilience* focused on very successful client-centric companies and traits that made those client-centric companies and their leaders successful. He noted that they were the same traits that made them successful in all aspects of the business, not just the way they interacted with their customers. "I think some people just have a higher-order sensibility. It's not just that they understand people are different and operate differently; it's much more than that. It's a nuance sensibility. It's not just about how they behave, it's how they think, how they process information, how they do decision making, or what are the rhythms of decision making. It's not all about behavioral issues. It's a thinking issue. It's much deeper. There are even cultural differences in aspiration, the way we look at information, the way we make decisions. Cultural sensibility is understanding how different cultures behave, think, and see things differently."

TALENT ORIENTATION: ACHIEVING THROUGH PEOPLE

In his book *Winning,* Jack Welch proclaims that a large part of his success as a transglobal leader could be attributed to his people management leadership. "Managing people was really what I did. After all, I didn't have the expertise to design jet engines, build CT scanners, or create a comedy program for NBC. . . . I believed the people part was how I could help GE the most." He also states unequivocally, "Without a doubt, the head of HR should be the second most important position in any organization. From the point of view of the CEO, the director of HR should be at least equal to the CFO."[4]

Transglobal leaders are personally engaged in talent development and consider people management a burning priority during all business and economic cycles. Our research shows that HR practices play a critical role in the success of transglobal leaders. They assume ownership of people practices within their organizations, and they are personally engaged in initiatives such as talent development, coaching, and succession planning. Transglobal leaders work very closely with HR, and oftentimes may commandeer and lead human resources initiatives themselves, relentlessly driving the connection between people and organizational performance.

"People who have been successful as leaders at Accenture are clearly the ones who care about coaching and developing their people," says Jill Smart, chief HR officer at Accenture. "Those who take the time to understand cultural differences as they collaborate on global teams are the ones most likely to rise to the top." According to Smart, Accenture has a virtual, global culture, in which senior leaders are located all over the world. She personally believes in leading by immersion. "If I'm traveling to a country that I haven't visited in a while, my standard protocol is to first have my team update me on the country dynamics, the economy, business environment, and ultimately, the HR indicators."

The people dimension ripples through every traditional leadership model. For decades, it has been proven over and over again that sustainable leadership is about motivating and inspiring people, about driving levels of engagement, and caring about people. Leadership literature differentiates behaviors of task orientation and people orientation that influence leader effectiveness. This might seem a bit intuitive and simplistic, especially since every leadership development or coaching program is focused on leaders' "softer" skills and their ability to integrate people management into their business strategies. However, our study confirmed that the people dimension is indeed an integral part of a successful leader's profile, and it is vital in driving business success. What we discovered in our research that is a bit different from these traditional leadership models is that transglobal leaders create enormous systemic leadership leverage when they take complete ownership of HR responsibilities such as talent sourcing and talent management, succession planning, performance management, diversity and inclusion, and employee engagement.

Transglobal leaders are acutely aware of the complexity of leading in a multicultural setting and the people dynamics in a world that is getting smaller and flatter. They also recognize that this complexity is compounded by the tsunami of social networks and communication forces that have been shaping the new workplace and influencing the axioms of leadership. Transglobal leaders have to constantly deal with generational and geographical challenges and the rapidly changing needs of a global society. Transglobal leaders are early adopters of technology and communication systems, leveraging tools to get closer to the people issues and then leading and educating by example. They tap into the human potential to drive change through the organization during any business transformation. In mergers and acquisitions, these leaders are most interested in the cultural aspects of the integration, a factor often overlooked by leaders who tend to work the economics of the deal and focus on the business versus the organizational elements and the people.

CASE STUDY

A Company Prospers Because of Its HR Focus

To better describe the talent orientation dimension, we would like to share a case study of a company that effectively weathered the 2008 economic recession by focusing on the human resources aspects of leadership. The company is Jones Lang LaSalle, a global leader in real estate, with a diverse executive leadership that focuses on driving business through people connections. Jones Lang LaSalle does business in over 60 countries with more than 40,000 employees dispersed across 150 cities. Four of the six executives who make up the company's Global Executive Committee live in countries outside their own. The strength of their leadership is manifested in their cultural sensitivity and their global connectivity, which enable them to make rapid critical decisions during all phases of the business cycle and across various geographies.

We identified a number of people who had joined the company from a competitor, and we asked them what they perceived to be the major differentiator between the two organizations. Two frequently mentioned factors were "access to leadership" and "ease of networking with people across borders." At Jones Lang LaSalle, they felt that they could much more easily reach out to senior leaders and engage in dialogue than they could at other firms where they had worked. Most of the Jones Lang LaSalle senior leaders, including the regional CEOs, sit in open plan six-packs amid other people, and they make it their business to get to know their talent.

The tone is set at the very top of the house by CEO Colin Dyer, a native of England who currently resides in Washington, DC. He speaks multiple European languages, and he is respected as an authentic transglobal leader. The company has tripled in size in the last seven years since he took over as CEO, and despite the fierce economic downturn, it has been highly profitable, maintaining its position as number one or two in virtually every market in which it operates. Additionally, it has been recognized by clients and outside organizations as the "Real Estate Company of Choice." As Dyer points out:

Confirming our claim to "First": Clients, industry peers, and independent organizations in all parts of the world recognize us with awards and honors. We won multiple awards at the Euromoney Awards and Best Place to Work titles in numerous markets all around the world. We were named to Ethisphere Institute's World's Most Ethical Companies list three years in a row, the only real estate company to receive such recognition. These and other honors confirmed our position as "First," the best in our business.

Dyer and his executive team consistently kept the people mandate in full view during up-and-down business cycles. Dyer, Lauralee Martin (chief financial and operating officer), and the regional CEOs forged forward with their business agenda while encouraging strategic foresight in dealing with the human issues at hand. Dyer paid particular attention to the human resources levers, and he was personally involved in advancing and proliferating HR agendas across the firm.

Some of the largest mandates, such as the development of the iconic "Shard" building in London (the London Bridge Tower), came about as a result of leaders from various geographies coming together as a team, without the benefit of an organizational structure to drive synergies.

Transglobal leaders successfully lead companies through unpredictable times by focusing the spotlight on the more predictable levers. In times of pressure and stress, communication and people strategies can go a long way in keeping the performance momentum on cruise control. The executives at Jones Lang LaSalle approached this in their own unique manner, but the common denominator was their focus on people and the relationships they fostered through a global web of interconnections. Some of the strategies that

Dyer's global group employed were:

- Identify key "franchise players" who are critical to the business and whose departure could engender huge losses for the franchise.
- Monitor the health and engagement levels of these individuals and the retention risks inherent in this core group.
- Safeguard human resources capabilities through robust succession planning and talent management strategies that are global in application.
- Upgrade and acquire talent from all parts of the world while aggressively addressing marginal players.
- Make business expansion and contraction decisions with a focus on culture and people, not just costs.

Exploiting one of the outcomes of the recession—a temporary cease-fire in the war for talent—Jones Lang LaSalle ramped up its external hiring both at lateral and raw-recruit levels. Recognizing that the competition for talent at the college campuses was weak, because the recession had hit the top financial institutions hard, the firm charged forward in bringing in A players from other firms as well as top students from reputable institutions. Dyer personally sent symbolic messages throughout the organization by taking a personal interest in attracting and bringing in highly qualified talent and selecting the people that he believed would build and enhance the diversity and talent muscle of the company. He always kept an eye out, however, for those he believed could, in time, move on to fill the growing need for talented global leaders. He spent hours in analyzing succession and attrition risks, and he reached out to the talent force, making them feel valued and invigorated. Communications through town halls and blogs were the norm. Connectedness became one of the five top global priorities, and people were recognized and rewarded for building global connections. Dyer and the executives we interviewed from other successful firms carry the human resources banner proudly and serve as exemplars for other aspiring transglobal leaders.

This case study highlights that transglobal leaders don't abandon the people element even in times of downturn. In fact, many cited that when times were tough, they worked hard at staying connected with their people. They became personally engaged in the development of talent, and they actively worked the succession planning and career development aspect of the talent equation.

Maria DiPietro, GE Capital EMEA, told us, "I am always talking to my team and those around me about their next career move. It is important that I stay connected to their personal aspirations and help them achieve them. I want people to feel they can be the best in this organization."

Transglobal leaders talk openly about the connection of the talent to the organization's performance. To them, people and performance go hand in hand. It is rare to hear transglobal leaders talk only about financial numbers. In fact, they usually respond negatively to a numbers-only approach to the business. They never underutilize human resources in the organizations. They are always looking for ways to stretch the talent and help individuals develop beyond what they thought was possible. They are sometimes seen, however, as soft and as focused only on people to the exclusion of business results. The truth, however, is quite the opposite. They are highly effective at achieving results, but they get the results through the people.

Again to highlight Gary Budzinski of HP Technology, he focused heavily on his people, and he saw results as being driven by his people. For 26 consecutive quarters, he was able to drive double-digit growth in his business—even when the economy was struggling. He has attributed this success to his deep caring and focus on the people in his organization.

The following summarizes what talent-oriented transglobal leaders do:

- They are personally engaged in talent development, and they maintain an intense interest in advancing the development of people.

- They have direct involvement with and ownership of succession planning initiatives. They safeguard talent risks through effective bench strength strategies.

- They hold themselves personally accountable for actions and outcomes.

- They keep people development and movement always at the core and center of strategy and business plans.

TALENT ORIENTATION IN ACTION

Steve Bertamini, who has held CEO positions in two great global companies—GE and Standard Chartered Bank—understands the importance of the talent orientation dimension. "The transition from GE to Standard Chartered Bank was made a lot easier because both companies had similar core values, and central to those values was a belief in people and the power of the team. At GE we learned to identify folks with strong leadership traits early in their careers. Leadership is about getting inspired by seeing other people grow and achieving things through other people. If you are not that sort of person, you will never be a leader. But to be a successful transglobal leader or to operate across cultures, you need a heightened sensitivity. Some of this heightened sensitivity is in your DNA, but some of it is coachable. But even if it's in your DNA, it still needs to be developed and refined. I have seen this heightened sensitivity in both genders and across all cultures, and it does not reside disproportionately in any particular group in my experience."

Jackie Wynn, who was VP of Imaging and Printing in the Public Sector Division of Hewlett-Packard and who has recently joined EMC as vice president, Global Residency Practice, was very successful in adapting to the global arena. She was at the forefront of diversity and inclusion at HP and had many years of embracing differences and building inclusive relationships across the HP world and within the teams she led. According to Wynn, "It's not about me. It's about the people that work with me. It's about helping them progress in their careers and mentoring a coaching relationship so people can continue to learn and grow. I make it my business to draw people out and learn about their hopes and dreams and see how I can help support them. This is what makes a workplace great and a place where people want to work. I know I am only as good as the people I work with. If they are excited about what they are doing and feel respected, they can contribute more at an individual and global level. . . . They will go the extra mile. Sometimes we don't always appreciate the global aspect of contributions."

CONCLUSION

Table 5.2 shows the Transglobal Leadership Matrix that summarizes the five essential characteristics described in this chapter.

While our survey and interviews validate these characteristics as essential for transglobal leaders, we would offer some caveats to consider. As mentioned earlier, any behavior or approach that is exaggerated or overused can and does have unintended consequences. We therefore share the following thoughts with transglobal leaders as they continue on the journey of global mastery:

Beware of going "native" and getting so immersed in a new culture that you can no longer see the world through a broad lens. On the flip side, watch out for becoming so broad that you become bland and see everything as the same and miss subtle nuances. Test yourself to ensure that you maintain focus, but don't become so rigid and outcome oriented that you forget how to be adaptable

Table 5.2 Transglobal Leadership Matrix at a Glance

Transglobal Leadership Dimension	Uncertainty Resilience: Building on Differences and Complexity	Team Connectivity: Integrating Across Boundaries	Pragmatic Flexibility: Adapting to Cultures	Perceptive Responsiveness: Acting on Intuition and Fact	Talent Orientation: Achieving Through People
Characteristic Behaviors	Read and analyze situations from multiple perspectives. Interpret things loosely and figuratively.	Adjust their activities to enhance the performance of others. Take responsibility when things go wrong.	Will adjust personal values to get the job done. Emphasize the needs of the work group.	Anticipate the changing needs of customers. Use negative feedback as an impetus for change and/or development.	Personally engaged in talent development. Get involved in and drive succession-planning initiatives.
Uncharacteristic Behaviors	Accentuate the potential costs and risks of innovation. Prefer continuity and stability in work situation.	See the world mainly in their own unique way. Expect others to redefine their roles in response to their needs.	Refuse to compromise. Emphasize norms, the formal group, and how things get done.	Lack sensitivity to different types of customers and their needs. Reward people in standardized ways; treat everyone the same.	Leave succession planning and talent management to the HR department.
Oriented Toward	Change and complexity.	Personal mastery and adaptation.	Consensus and action.	Recognizing the unique characteristics of individuals.	Tapping human potential.
Talks About	Strategic vision, opportunities, and goals.	Collaboration, support, and what's in it for the team.	Constructive compromises; higher-order solutions.	Overarching frameworks that allow for diversity.	Connection between people and organizational performance.

(continued on next page)

Table 5.2 Transglobal Leadership Matrix at a Glance *(continued)*

Transglobal Leadership Dimension	Uncertainty Resilience: Building on Differences and Complexity	Team Connectivity: Integrating Across Boundaries	Pragmatic Flexibility: Adapting to Cultures	Perceptive Responsiveness: Acting on Intuition and Fact	Talent Orientation: Achieving Through People
Responds Negatively To	Linear, overly detailed analysis.	Egotism; acting out of personal self-interests.	Power-oriented and conventional thinking.	Constraining rules and rigid approaches.	An exclusive focus on the numbers.
Not Likely To	Put things in "boxes."	Act selfishly or at others' expense.	Dismiss others' views or be unyielding.	Take a one-size-fits-all approach.	Overlook or waste the organization's talent.
Impact on Organizational Culture	Achievement norms.	Humanistic-encouraging norms.	Achievement norms.	Self-actualizing norms.	Constructive norms.
Comes Across As:	Confident.	Doing the right thing.	Tolerant.	Astute and discerning.	People oriented.
But Can Be Seen As:	Reckless.	Overly accommodating.	Unprincipled.	Inconsistent or unfair.	Soft, idealistic, faddish.
Leadership Strength	Create meaning out of ambiguity.	Act based on the needs of others and the organization.	Adjust to different approaches, perspectives, situations.	Treat people as individuals.	Achieve effectiveness through people.

or lose sight of the people around you. Remain challenged by new experiences, or else you run the risk of becoming bored and you will lack the motivation to follow through. Remember that local innovations and breakthrough approaches are essential, but you can run the risk of too much customization that can erode the value of your organization's global supply chain. Finally, remember to constantly test if innovation and product development are truly global or local; know how to make the distinction, and act accordingly.

If you want to know whether you have the makings of a transglobal leader and embody the global mindset, reflect on the matrix (Figure 5.1) and see what applies to you and what causes you concern. Most of all read Part III of this book. Compare your scores from Chapter 1 to our transglobal leadership results. Test yourself and your organization for your overall transglobal leadership capability. Becoming a transglobal leader is a continual journey toward developing these behaviors, and many leaders don't have all of them. The good news is that, for the most part, these behaviors can be developed, and we will discuss this in Part III.

CHAPTER 6

Traditional Diversity Versus Transglobal Diversity: The New Order and Debate

*To be a successful global leader, you must be a "builder"—
you must grow the business, you must build capabilities
and build an organization that can solve its own
problems. Truly embracing diversity is a key tenet of a
"builder." The command-and-control or do-it-yourself
leader does not tend to build these capabilities. Building
networks globally requires embracing diversity and
tapping into all of the varied and diverse capabilities of
the organization.*

—DAVID MAISTER, AUTHOR AND ONE OF
THE WORLD'S LEADING AUTHORITIES ON
THE MANAGEMENT OF GLOBAL AND LOCAL
PROFESSIONAL SERVICES FIRMS[1]

Our research results are consistent with Maister's sentiment that building a successful global organization, whether in an emerging market or in a high-growth environment, requires a concerted focus on diversity and inclusion. The most experienced transglobal leaders have moved from a conscious state of seeking diverse talent to a more natural or subconscious state of competence in building and working with heterogeneous teams. They are not afraid of differences, and they are able to deal with all the diversity that a global environment presents.

Three noteworthy findings in our study related to diversity are:

- Transglobal leaders recognize the significance of diversity and inclusion in a corporate ecosystem and their relevance in today's global markets.

- Transglobal leaders can deal with differences on multiple fronts, including diverse customers, employees, suppliers, and other stakeholders.

- Results for men and women are similar on most of the survey's items with few differences, which implies that women are as suited as men for transglobal leadership roles.

This chapter defines traditional diversity and juxtaposes it with diversity within a global context using the five dimensions of a successful transglobal leader to frame and structure a global diversity model. Through examples and stories from transglobal leaders who are the exemplars in setting the tone and context for their teams, we will define diversity and describe how leaders can leverage institutional, cultural, gender, generational, and other differences to unleash the potential in teams and achieve breakthrough thinking.

This chapter also sets out a simple path for transglobal leaders who may be struggling with this topic, and it shows them how to adopt an enriched global mindset that can alter the course for them and their organizations.

Appreciating diversity today is often translated as being the "right" thing to do, which is typically a euphemism for "politically correct." We have found that diversity as it is understood by local leaders is not just coincidentally or marginally different from diversity as described by our successful transglobal leaders. Instead, it is remarkably different. Table 6.1 summarizes these differences.

WHAT IS THE TRADITIONAL ARGUMENT FOR DIVERSITY, AND WHY DOES IT MATTER?

Diversity takes on different meanings in different countries, and the "mix" can vary from place to place. For instance, in the United States, racial groups are defined and very well understood by all. In the United States, workplace diversity is defined using the following criteria: gender, race, ethnicity, age, mental and physical abilities and characteristics, and sexual orientation.

Table 6.1   Traditional Diversity Versus the New Order of Global Diversity

Traditional Diversity	New Order of Global Diversity
Prevalent and focused primarily in the United States and driven across borders by U.S. leaders	Embraced globally and by all leaders irrespective of location
Defined narrowly by race, gender, age, and other physical characteristics and demographics	Defined broadly to reflect culture, inclusion, respect, and engagement
Artificially enforced by law: affirmative action in the United States, quotas for boards in certain European countries	Naturally adopted and appreciated by successful transglobal leaders across the globe without legal mandates
Outcomes achieved as a result of goals, objectives, and established metrics	Outcomes achieved naturally without prompts and as a result of leader intuition
Defined as "diversity and inclusion"	Defined as "inclusive diversity"
Driven by a chief diversity officer or someone in HR to drive the agenda	An integral part of the business and embedded in the core processes of the firm
Defined differently in each local market	Defined consistently in every market

The term *affirmative action* was first established and used in the United States through an executive order issued in 1965 by President Lyndon Johnson. This order required federal contractors to hire without regard to race, religion, or national origin. Since then, several modifications have been made, and affirmative action plans have taken various forms in several countries. However, in some nations where there are laws on racial equality, affirmative action plans are rendered illegal as they tend to show preferential treatment toward a particular group.

Many universities around the world establish admission "quotas" that give preferential treatment to one or more diverse groups, typically those who have been historically disadvantaged because of race, gender, disability, native or aboriginal background, age, or religion. In India, government and educational institutions have established quotas for jobs and college admissions to include more people from the lower or "scheduled" caste in an effort to correct past discrimination practices.

The issue of gender imbalance at the top of organizations has created a movement in a few European nations where change is being legislated through regulation and government mandates. Several governments have decided that radical action is required to increase the number of women in the boardroom and executive suite. Norway passed a law in 2003 that obliged all publicly listed firms to reserve 40 percent of the seats on their boards for women by 2008. Spain passed a similar law in 2007; France early in 2011. The Netherlands is working on one. On July 6, 2011, the European Parliament passed a resolution calling for EU-wide legislation stipulating that at least 40 percent of seats on listed companies' supervisory boards be reserved for women by 2020. There is a compelling and clear business case for diversity in many parts of the world. The traditional debate has, over the years, continued to produce empirical evidence that companies with diverse boards and executive committees tend to produce better results.

Several studies have shown that diverse teams have a far greater chance of achieving high performance than do homogeneous teams, particularly if led by a strong leader.[2] Research by Catalyst, McKinsey & Company, and others shows that there is clearly a positive impact of gender diversity on company performance. McKinsey's *Women Matter* study established a link between gender diversity in the top management positions of a company and its performance (see Figure 6.1).[3] McKinsey extended the original U.S. study to Brazil, Russia, India, and China (BRIC) and found similar results.

Catalyst also studied the leadership and gender gap in India and found that companies with the highest representation of women in their top management teams experienced, on average, 34 to 35 percent better financial performance than companies with the lowest women's representation. A *McKinsey Quarterly* report states, "Women start careers in business and other professions with the same level of intelligence, education, and commitment as men. Yet comparatively few reach the top echelons."

It is clear that the link between diversity and performance is strong, and companies with more women in their executive teams

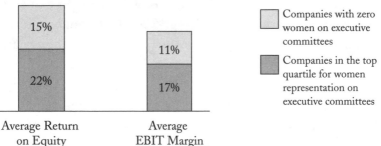

Figure 6.1 The Higher Financial Performance of Companies with Higher Proportions of Women in Their Executive Committees

Note: Countries covered are United Kingdom, France, Germany, Spain, Sweden, Norway, Brazil, Russia, India, China.

Source: Adapted from corporate websites and McKinsey analysis.

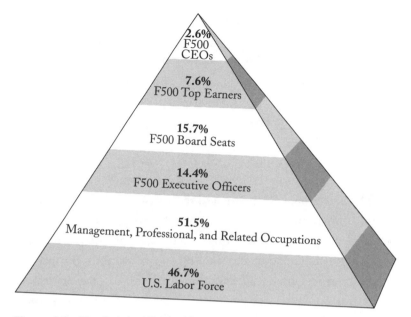

Figure 6.2 The Catalyst Pyramid

Sources:
Catalyst research, July 12, 2011.
Catalyst, *2010 Catalyst Census: Fortune 500 Women Board Directors.*
Catalyst, *2010 Catalyst Census: Fortune 500 Women Executive Officers and Top Earners.*
Bureau of Labor Statistics, 2010 Current Population Survey, "Employed Persons by Detailed Occupation, Sex, Race, and Hispanic or Latino Ethnicity."
Bureau of Labor Statistics, 2010 Current Population Survey, "Employment Status of the Civilian Noninstitutional Population by Age, Sex, and Race."

perform better; however, women have not climbed the leadership ladder at the same pace as men. Only 2.6 percent of Fortune 500 company CEOs are women (see Figure 6.2).

What is also clear is that CEOs and senior transglobal leaders recognize that diversity and innovation are important in driving a growth agenda. Furthermore, a vast number of executives cite a shortage of global talent as a critical challenge in the future. This shortage of global talent makes diversity an even greater priority for global businesses. In the 2010 PricewaterhouseCoopers (PwC) study of over 1,200 CEOs in 69 countries, it was found that two of the top three focal points driving strategic change internationally were talent and innovation. The study shows that talent is now at the top of CEO agendas across all regions.[4]

THE NEW ORDER OF GLOBAL DIVERSITY: A SHIFT FROM THE TRADITIONAL ORDER

What started as a business imperative is now evolving into a natural phenomenon, as noted by transglobal leaders.

The new global debate related to diversity extends far beyond the traditional meanings and metrics. It extends beyond gender, race, age, and other demographics. Most importantly, it extends beyond the diversity of customers, suppliers, and employees. Successful transglobal leaders embrace differences in every aspect of the business and every aspect of human values and principles. Transglobal leaders not only embrace differences but also naturally and organically create an aura and culture of respect, inclusion, and engagement. Transglobal leaders embody a global mindset.

The examples in the case studies from transglobal leaders define the evolution and role of diversity in a global context.

Michael Vavakis, group head of human resources for Lend Lease, told us:

> We are a very inclusive organization, and we celebrate "all the ways in which we differ"—a phrase well known within Lend Lease. Whilst we have gender targets, we see diversity and inclusion as far more than a gender issue. We look for people with different life experiences, different perspectives, and different behavioral styles, as well as a mix of gender and race to get a diversity of thought, which we see as critical to the health of the organization as we grow globally—all the ways in which we differ, that's what we celebrate.[5]

It is experience in a global setting that has shaped the thinking of the transglobal leaders. Their beliefs and behaviors are defined and refined as they recognize the power and synergies created through experience and immersion in different societies, cultures, and geographies.

CASE STUDY

Lauralee Martin, Chief Financial and Operating Officer for Jones Lang LaSalle (JLL)

Lauralee Martin recounted for us her business travels that have taken her to numerous European and Asian countries and her evolution from enjoying the new countries as a tourist to appreciating the connections with new and varied cultures within these countries.

"We, as leaders at JLL, chose connectivity as one of our top five priorities to advance our global delivery of best service to our clients through relationships around the world. We delve deeply into the cultural expectations, attitudes, and norms of the countries where we do business, with a goal of mutual respect. In a recent visit to Indonesia, we all dressed in Indonesian batik, and when we were in India, all our senior executives from various parts of the world wore the traditional hand-woven *kurta* (Indian attire from the Gandhian days).

"I find that meeting people on their terms and in their comfort zone enriches the experience for me and creates longer-lasting relationships. People who respect and influence other people bring out the best in these people."

Martin grew up in a homogeneous environment in the United States, but she enjoyed the outdoors, loved to read and travel, and went to London to study when she was 20. She said that over the years, her travel and exposure to diverse groups has caused her to focus on outcomes rather than on how these outcomes are achieved. "The richness of global diversity is to let people enjoy doing work within their personal and cultural context. You can get to the same answer in many different ways, and oftentimes the outcomes are far superior in quality and the service delivered to clients is greatly enhanced as a result."[6]

As noted above, diversity at the board level is proving to be a differentiator for companies. For instance, a Catalyst survey revealed that companies with three or more women on their boards tend to have better financial results than companies with fewer or no women directors.[7]

The case study about Sheila Penrose reflects the power of diversity from her perspective.

CASE STUDY

Sheila Penrose, Chair of the Board of Directors for Jones Lang LaSalle

In addition to chairing the board of Jones Lang LaSalle, Sheila Penrose serves on the boards of McDonald's and the technology company DataCard Group. She served on the advisory board of Catalyst for more than a decade, and she cofounded and cochairs the Corporate Leadership Center, which provides leadership development for senior executives in major corporations at key inflexion points in their careers. In her 30-year career, she has served in academic roles, in economic advisory roles for the U.K. Treasury Department, and executive advisory roles for the Boston Consulting Group. She was the president of Northern Trust's global corporate bank and served for seven years as the first and only woman on the bank's management committee.

"As a corporate director, one of your most important responsibilities is to make sure the talent within the organization is developing well—and that includes diverse talent in every sense because today's global markets are diverse."[8]

Having served on multiple global boards, Penrose believes that board composition is critical and directly related to its success and ultimately to the success of the company. Global companies that are U.S. based must represent the countries in which they conduct business.

"When you have a global board, it sends a message that you understand a global company and you seek to develop talent globally. The claim is always made that finding women, minorities, and foreign-based board members is difficult. It is if you use familiar networks and expect to find new and different talent. You have to challenge the notion that a sitting CEO is the best candidate for a board seat and decide instead what the attributes are that are needed, not just the titles. If you rely on personal networks, you're likely to get more of what you already have."[9]

Penrose benefits from having been on both sides of the fence, and she shares her growth and learning from these experiences. "One of the most valuable development experiences I had as an executive was to serve simultaneously as a non-executive director of another public company. I sat at the 'other side of the table' and saw issues differently. I learned different business models, and I saw different role models and different ways of executing effectively."[10]

As talent shortages become chronic, the only way out is to expand labor pools and to create a global mindset. Japan, for instance, continues to cultivate a rather homogeneous labor market, particularly in comparison with markets in China, India, Hong Kong, and other Asian countries. It is predicted that labor shortfalls in Japan will be acute unless the country changes its workforce practices. Very few women in Japan return to work once they bear children, and the turnover of female workers is high. One way to address the labor shortage would be to begin to develop ways to make the workplace friendly for Japanese moms.

CASE STUDY

Accenture

Accenture has recognized the talent challenge in Japan, and it is addressing it in several ways. Pamela Craig, Accenture's chief financial officer, has maintained especially close ties with Accenture women in Japan. She played a key role in sponsoring the promotion of Accenture's first woman executive in that market, and she helped create the company's first women's program there. Today, Accenture has a number of senior female executives in Japan—with a pipeline of talented senior managers.

Another example of Accenture's commitment to global diversity is reflected in the appointment of Harsh Manglik as cochairman and geography managing director of Accenture in India. Manglik, although a native of India, had spent 35 years in the United States. But when asked to serve as chairman in India, he was comfortable taking on the cultural and physical displacement required, not just because of his own extensive global travel but also because of his confidence in Accenture's commitment to help him be effective in his role.

Accenture believes in the power of leaders teaching leaders. Senior executives train others in the tools needed to build confident individuals. In one course—Leading a

> Diverse Workforce—transglobal and local leaders help exec-
> utives reexamine their beliefs with respect to diversity, better
> understand how to leverage and promote an inclusive culture,
> and use this refreshed perspective as a basis for developing
> concrete diversity plans for their scope of accountability.

Although examples such as the ones described in the case studies are beginning to reflect an appreciation for diversity by certain companies and executives in many parts of the world, such thinking is not yet commonplace, and there isn't a consistent definition for diversity outside the United States. American companies have maintained that inclusion is as critical as diversity, but most of the world outside the United States remains focused primarily on gender diversity.

The most recently adopted abbreviation in this arena, particularly in the United States, is D&I, which stands for *diversity and inclusion*. Not long ago, companies took pride in claiming the ability to hire and retain a diverse workforce. The notion of inclusion was added more recently when it became evident that hiring and retaining a diverse workforce wasn't adequate and that diversity needed to be complemented by an inclusive and constructive culture. The terms *diversity* and *inclusion* are often bandied about as synonyms. Andrés Tapia, an expert in this area, has stated that while they relate to the same ultimate goal, they are in no way synonymous. "*Diversity* is the mix. *Inclusion* is making the mix work."[11]

Notwithstanding the legalities and the impositions placed on companies, we found that sound leadership behaviors consistent with the dimensions identified in Chapter 4 can be a significant force in driving diversity, fairness, trust, and loyalty into global corporate ecosystems. Our study has taken diversity and inclusion to a different level. Intuitively, we can all agree that it is conceivable to have a highly diverse workforce or team, but without an inclusive leader, team members may not necessarily achieve high levels of engagement or commitment or perform at their peak. Similarly, highly inclusive leaders who lead only homogeneous teams may not trigger creativity or breakthrough thinking, and the lack of diverse perspectives can stifle innovative ideas and growth.

Transglobal leaders, on the other hand, nurture and sustain not just a diverse but also an inclusive mindset. Transglobal leaders do not separate diversity from inclusion: they believe that these are inseparable values that cannot be detached if superior performance and outstanding business results are to be achieved in a global world. In the new order of life, the "and" in D&I is superfluous. Transglobal leaders embrace *inclusive diversity*; this plays a critical role in the success of these leaders, and it can be instrumental to both the innovativeness and adaptability of their businesses.

The framework in Figure 6.3 and its examples of inclusive diversity behaviors reflect how transglobal leaders respond, adapt, and sustain practices and behaviors that will endure the complexities of the changing work environment and withstand the test of time.

As noted at the beginning of this chapter, our research findings related to gender differences revealed that men and women responded similarly to the Transglobal Survey items; they are

Figure 6.3 Transglobal Leadership Inclusive Diversity Framework

equally capable of climbing the transglobal leadership ladder. This finding has significant implications for CEOs and leaders who are dealing with talent shortages, as well as for women who are aspiring to penetrate the global C-suite glass ceiling.

Other significant findings from our study and interviews that directly relate to inclusive diversity are that transglobal leaders:

- Are actively inclusive and seek out divergent perspectives.

- Attempt to speak multiple languages or attempt to learn and speak languages other than their own; however, women are slightly more inclined than men to make an effort to speak in a nonnative language.

- Bring people into teams from widely diverse backgrounds, and will adjust their activities and preferences to enhance the performance of the team members.

- Are extremely comfortable working with diverse people in diverse settings, and they encourage connections and collaboration within and across teams and geographies.

- Are curious and reflective learners who are on a mission of discovery. Rather than rely on their own views, they seek multiple viewpoints and scout for new wisdom among people from diverse backgrounds and cultures.

- Nurture and take a personal interest in their people regardless of who or where they are; they are therefore successful at attracting and holding on to diverse talent.

- Have the innate or learned ability to build and inspire diverse teams.

Although the characteristics of transglobal leaders are inherent in both men and women and both are likely to succeed in a global environment, women continue to remain underrepresented in executive suites and corporate boardrooms. The 2010 McKinsey study mentioned above reported that the highest representation of women on boards is in Norway, with 32 percent, and the lowest is in India, with 5 percent. Ironically, more than half the students who are in the top colleges in India are women; however, very few make it to the top of companies.[12] Only 2 percent of the executive committees in India include women members. China continues to face similar challenges in promoting women into higher levels: only 6 percent of its corporate boards and only 8 percent of its executive committees include women members. Despite the push to elevate the diversity agenda and promote women and minorities in the United States, only 15 percent of its corporate boards and only 14 percent of its executive committees include women members (see Figure 6.4).

THE ROLE AND SIGNIFICANCE OF DIVERSITY IN THE TRANSGLOBAL LEADERSHIP MODEL

The characteristics of the emerging workforce have changed significantly, calling for leaders to be increasingly flexible, vibrant,

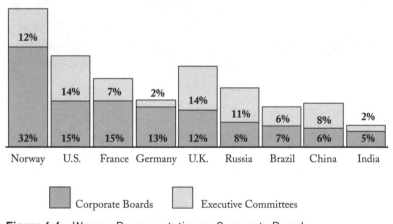

Figure 6.4 Women Representation on Corporate Boards and Executive Committees in 2010.
In 2010, women are still underrepresented in boards of corporations, although improvement has been seen in some countries.

Source: Adapted from corporate websites and McKinsey analysis.

progressive, and ultrasensitive to how they are being perceived and accepted by their employees. Virtually every leader surveyed by us talked about changing market dynamics, demographic shifts, and the challenges of leading in a rapidly growing multicultural labor market. The emerging workforce is vastly diverse, people issues are essentially unpredictable, and social norms are constantly evolving at an unfathomable pace.

The world is getting smaller, not simpler. In fact, diversity is prevalent in almost every organization that does business internationally or globally. Some organizations, through mergers and acquisitions, become diverse overnight and don't know how to deal with it. Others get a new customer in another part of the world and struggle to figure out how to best engage that customer for the long haul. Transglobal leaders recognize that global diversity is an inherent part of doing business today and it will become an increasingly significant factor in the future. Transglobal leaders are not afraid of diversity; in fact, they actively embrace and enjoy the differences and expanded thinking that these differences create.

We found that the characteristics of the transglobal leaders and their deeply held convictions set them apart from others in driving the diversity agenda almost effortlessly through their organizations. All five dimensions of transglobal leadership serve to enhance the elements of inclusion, selflessness, and connectivity, and they bring inclusive diversity into sharper focus. The three that are most distinct are Perceptive Responsiveness, Uncertainty Resilience, and Talent Orientation.

PERCEPTIVE RESPONSIVENESS: ACTING ON INTUITION AND FACT

Transglobal leaders are skilled at reading people; they have good antennae and are sensitive to individuals' cultural and social norms, behaviors, and biases. They are almost disdainful of noninclusive behaviors, and they will not condone or promote individuals who are narrow-minded or those who view diversity as an agenda rather than a value. In contrast, many local leaders, even today, see diversity and inclusion as impositions that are externally forced on them and as "politically correct" and "right" actions that will serve only to make them and their organizations look good and feel good.

Research has shown that building and inspiring diverse teams takes effort. Homogeneous groups may be easier to manage and under a leader with average skills may perform better, as demonstrated in a number of studies. We have seen many local leaders who have tended to take the easy road and gravitate to homogeneous groups. It is commonly assumed that diverse teams are better than homogenous teams when it comes to generating innovation and new ideas. This assumption, however, is coming under increasing scrutiny. Studies at INSEAD and Harvard show that the potential benefits of diverse teams do not automatically come to the fore. In fact, under average leadership, diverse teams tend to generate fewer innovative ideas than homogeneous teams[13] (see Figure 6.5a). High-capability leaders seem to be required for diverse teams to perform effectively (see Figure 6.5b).

It is the differences in the makeup of the diverse team that generate the barriers to breakthrough innovation. The variety of decision-making processes, communication styles, and dynamics get in the way when the group is led by a leader who has only average levels of perceptive responsiveness. However, a team with a skilled leader has the potential to be a high-performing team. With higher levels of understanding and involvement, a transglobal leader of a diverse team is more likely to generate breakthrough innovation than a transglobal leader of a homogeneous team. Doing so is not easy, as explained by Clayton Daley in the following sidebar. Nevertheless, these transglobal leaders are big believers in having geographically dispersed leadership versus headquarters-only leadership to drive their agendas forward.

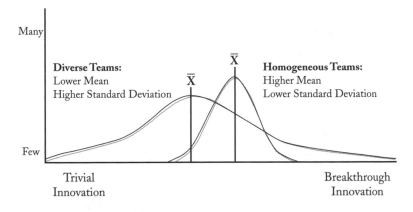

Figure 6.5a Leading Diverse Teams: Achieving Breakthrough Innovation

Source: J. Stewart Black, PhD, professor at INSEAD, Leading for Results: Making the Best Out of Diverse Teams presentation slides, September 2005. Used with permission.

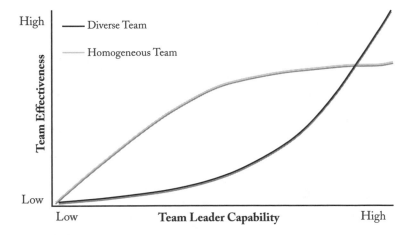

Figure 6.5b Leading Diverse Teams: Achieving Team Effectiveness

Source: J. Stewart Black, PhD, professor at INSEAD, Leading for Results: Making the Best Out of Diverse Teams presentation slides, September 2005. Used with permission.

Clayton Daley, retired Vice Chairman
and CFO of Procter & Gamble

Clayton Daley told us, "Managing diverse teams is a lot more work. It's more challenging. At P&G, we put a lot of focus on it. Of course, when it comes to diversity, people instantly think about themselves. They think we're talking about them. But I have always viewed it more broadly. It covers multiple cultures, experiences, and styles. If a company has 60 percent of its business outside of the United States, then I would say that 60 percent of the leadership should be outside the United States."

Daley also believes that diverse groups tend to do much better than homogeneous groups during a cross-cultural merger or acquisition. "When you go into different countries, a lot of what is done is based on local business practices, local cultures, and the local ways of doing things. I actually believe that companies with different nationalities involved tend to be more accepting of integrating cultures during a merger than homogeneous groups such as an all-American team."[14]

Daley's statements, once again, show that transglobal leaders see diversity and inclusion through a more perceptive and different lens than do traditional leaders. They consider inclusive diversity to be a core business and personal value. They view the practice of inclusive diversity as the respectful thing to do, not just the right thing. They cherish differences in people, and they include people of various backgrounds in their circles, both social and business. They are convinced that diverse teams will enable their success and that inclusive diversity is and will be at the heart of innovation and growth.

In the same way that unsighted people or the hearing-impaired develop their other senses to a far higher degree than the average person, transglobal leaders have honed senses that help them tune into and clearly perceive their new environments and the people within them. They recognize that cultures are different—people do not interpret events and behaviors the same way, and expectations can vary widely.

Inclusive diversity is also about understanding and respecting cultural differences and appreciating the behavioral nuances that vary from country to country. Transglobal leaders inherently understand that the new order of diversity is not only a mix but also a major shift to inclusion, with a heavy emphasis on seeking out and showing respect for others' perspectives. They will hire the best and brightest no matter who they are or where in the world they live or come from.

UNCERTAINTY RESILIENCE: BUILDING ON DIFFERENCES AND COMPLEXITY

Working with diverse teams promotes uncertainty and ambiguity. Cultural, racial, gender, generational, religious, social, familial, and other differences can generate behaviors that are not necessarily well understood by most leaders. Not everything is likely to line up neatly. Though far from perfect, transglobal leaders acknowledge and respect differences and make every attempt to learn from them.

Several studies have been conducted highlighting cultural differences. Psychologist Richard Nisbett's *The Geography of Thought* is a brilliant study showing how Asians and Westerners think differently.[15] Nisbett's research clearly demonstrates that educational and work environments are enriched with people of different backgrounds. For example, the cognitive orientations and skills of East Asians can be quite different than those of others. Therefore, it would seem highly likely that their presence would enrich groups in a variety of settings.

In one study, American and Chinese children were shown three pictures depicting a child, a man, and a woman. Then they were asked to choose two pictures that were alike and to explain their choices. The majority of the Chinese children chose to group the child with the woman, explaining that the child was the mother's responsibility. The Americans mainly chose the man and the woman, with the explanation that they were both adults. This result suggests that Chinese have a tendency to group objects by relationships while Americans prefer to group objects by categories. A similar study showed that Australians favored grouping objects together by shape, while Japanese predominantly grouped them by the material they were made of.

Globalization is not about homogenizing cultures but about exposing a greater number of people to more people from different cultures. It is in this context that the demand for transglobal leaders with a strong tolerance for ambiguity, who can bridge cultural and communication gaps, has never been greater. Many leaders fear the loss of homogeneous relationships, and they fear behaviors and attitudes that are different from their own. These leaders need to work hard to embrace such differences and not reject them as foreign or threatening. Transglobal leaders thrive on the differences and welcome the fresh angles that diverse perspectives can offer.

Talent Orientation: Achieving Through People

Transglobal leaders are personally involved in the development and growth of talent. They immerse themselves in people processes, one of which is building a diverse workforce.

Transglobal leaders are naturally wired to value and recognize the power of diverse teams. The leaders we interviewed cited several examples of their personal involvement in discovering and nurturing diverse talent and fostering a culture of *inclusive diversity*. Their focus and interests extend beyond the executive layer and into the deeper crevices of the talent pipeline of next-generation, high-potential global leaders.

Andrés Tapia states, "Diversity as solely a human resources thing will wither on the vine."[16] We found during our interviews that our transglobal leaders relied on HR or their chief diversity officers primarily for creating the infrastructure—the tools and systems—to enable the acquisition and development of diverse talent. However, they personally drove the people agenda in various ways. Examples of their involvement include:

- Displaying an unwavering commitment to building and sustaining a diverse enterprise in all geographies

- Actively role modeling inclusive behaviors and building diverse teams within their own reporting structures

- Ensuring HR processes and initiatives (such as succession planning, talent acquisition, promotion, career planning, etc.) have integrated diversity objectives and then holding leaders and HR accountable for delivering on these objectives

- Listening to multiple views and perspectives and encouraging idea generation from all sources, regardless of background

The success stories that follow further reflect the care and level of prominence that transglobal leaders place in driving diversity and inclusion initiatives and best practices within the workplace.

DIVERSITY AND TRANSGLOBAL LEADERSHIP SUCCESS STORIES

The bar has been set high by many companies, mostly influenced by the tone at the top. Here are just a few examples of companies that continue to gain recognition for their diversity strategies and initiatives. These are companies whose leaders are migrating from the traditional world of diversity into the more inclusive world of dealing with diverse groups. These stories demonstrate exemplary initiatives that have moved these companies further along the continuum toward inclusive diversity:

- Earlier, we discussed the progressive work done by Accenture in Asian markets. Accenture is also well known for its generational communications and for diversity programs involving all age groups. Chairman of the Board of Directors William Green has stated, "Diversity and inclusiveness are years past being a program; they're a state of the mind at our company. And we will take the best people on any terms we can get them, and we work very hard to do that, particularly in the service industry, where your assets have legs and can leave the building. The thing that has become true in the last several years is that diversity and inclusiveness have become one of the characteristics of a high-performing company. If you intend to compete in the United States or on the global stage, you have to be able to embrace it in every dimension; . . . it's a journey, not a destination, we will never be satisfied."[17]

- PricewaterhouseCoopers (PwC) is often recognized as a top company for working families. It is noted and recognized for its family-friendly policies and for the investments it has made in work–life balance strategies. Some of its investments include implementing best-of-class parental-leave programs, such as:

  - Three weeks off with pay to new fathers to take any time during the first year

  - A national launch of the Mentor Moms program, an online community connecting new mothers or mothers-to-be with experienced PwC moms who have efficiently juggled work and motherhood

- The Full Circle program, which allows parents to step out of the workforce to properly play that role full time while retaining training privileges so they can return to work

- The Special Needs Caregiver Circle program for employees dealing with special-needs children and disabilities within the family, giving them access to shared experiences and resources through a web-based portal dedicated to caregiving

Additionally, PwC has an extensive coaching program to develop high-potential diverse talent for partnership in the firm. This program uses both internal and external coaches, and it has been instrumental in achieving more diversity at the partner level of PwC. The extensive engagement of senior leadership in the development of diverse talent is quite impressive.

Investment in these programs continued through the 2008 to 2009 economic downturn. Chairman of PwC International Ltd. Dennis Nally stated, "Bad times don't last; good people do. I'm convinced that companies [recognized for diversity] are organizations that really recognize the critical role that diversity plays in leveraging the productivity and, importantly, the loyalty of their workforce—they continue to invest in diversity."[18]

- Kaiser Permanente is ranked number one on the DiversityInc Top Companies for Diversity in 2011. It has the most diverse board of directors and management, especially the top three levels of management, that DiversityInc has seen. Half of the board members are black, Latino, and Asian, and 36 percent of the board members are women. Its top level of management is 38 percent black, Latino, and Asian, and 25 percent women.

Kaiser has exceptionally strong diversity leadership from its chairman and CEO, George Halvorson, who leads the National Diversity Council. What makes Kaiser remarkable is the consistency of its diversity management efforts, as well as the alignment between diversity in the workplace and diversity in the customer base. For example, the organization's Institute for Culturally Competent Care and the nine Centers of Excellence are making significant strides in eradicating healthcare disparities for blacks, Latinos, Asians, people with disabilities, and immigrants.[19]

- For more than a decade, Deloitte LLP and its subsidiaries (Deloitte) has been recognized for its leadership in implementing diversity and inclusion leading practices. *Working Mother* magazine ranked Deloitte in the top 5 "Best Companies for Multicultural Women" list in 2011. For nine consecutive years Deloitte has made *DiversityInc* magazine's "Top 50 Best Companies for Diversity" list.[20] The organization has stated, "Globalization and technology are creating organizations with fewer rungs and more options for how, when, and where work gets done. The workforce is profoundly different too. From gender to generations, it is more diverse in every sense of the word. Workers' needs, expectations, and definitions of success don't match those of the homogeneous workforce of days gone by. The result is that the career ladder is splintering. The corporate lattice is emerging. A lattice metaphor more aptly describes the changing world of work. Careers zig and zag. Work is what you do, not where you go."

    Deloitte's work in moving toward a latticed, highly networked, and incredibly diverse organization has been the topic of many written pieces on leadership and diversity. Deborah DeHaas, vice chairman and central region managing partner of Deloitte LLP, describes it as "connecting across the world, connecting across clients, and connecting through influence rather than authority. One of our core values is embracing diversity and inclusion. We develop better solutions for our clients when we bring together diverse teams who offer a variety of backgrounds, experiences, ideas, and diverse thinking patterns. When client service teams are formed at Deloitte, we take a step back and look at the composition and will make changes in order to construct a diverse team of our qualified professionals who have the right experiences and skills to serve our clients. We also understand that both women and men offer unique perspectives to solving business challenges, and we make a conscious effort to provide them with the right opportunities to lead client teams."[21]

- McDonald's has also received commendations for its work on diversity on a global level. Pat Harris, global chief diversity officer, defines diversity as a "broad mix of ideas, opinions, backgrounds, and life experiences, in addition to the traditional measures like race and gender."[22] In 2009, McDonald's global workforce of over 1.6 million employees, from crew members in restaurants to the CEO, was composed of 62 percent women and over 60 percent non-Caucasians.

  Jim Skinner, company vice chairman and CEO, has stated, "McDonald's has an unwavering commitment to inclusion and diversity in our workforce, among our franchisees, and with our suppliers—in the United States and everywhere else in the world where we do business."[23] Race and ethnicity play a key role at McDonald's, where African American entrepreneurs are sought out for franchise operations. The term *zebra* or *salt-and-pepper partnerships* has been used to describe white investors who worked alongside their African American franchisees running inner-city restaurants.

Don Thompson, president and chief operating officer of McDonald's USA, is an African American responsible for directing McDonald's global strategy and operations for its 32,000 restaurants in 117 countries. Diversity at McDonald's starts with the board of directors, the members of which are also a highly diverse group of executives.

Sheila Penrose, a director for McDonald's, whom we referred to earlier in the chapter as a successful transglobal leader, made this comment to us in an interview:

> As a corporate director, one of your most important responsibilities is to make sure the talent in the organization is being developed well. Organizations committed to developing their high-potential talent find that women and minorities face barriers: they are not as well networked in their organizations; they may not have as many mentors; and often they don't have active advocates. Most of all, they may not have role models— and it's tough to "be what you can't see" ahead of you![24]

- Coauthor Peter Barge, the retired Asia Pacific CEO of Jones Lang LaSalle, is an Australian who had worked overseas for 20 years with two assignments in Asia and two in the United States. At the time he was appointed CEO of the Asia Pacific region, of the 12 branches that were in Asian countries, only one was run by a local Asian. Most of the other branches were run by senior leaders (all of them men) who were expats from Western countries.

  Peter effected a change in leadership that brought with it a complete change in attitude and mindset. Diversity became front and center as career moves took on a multicultural dynamic. Very quickly, the composition of leaders and teams started to change. More locals were given the opportunity to rise to the executive ranks, and within the span of just three years, locals (two of them women) were running most of the countries. Several countries had received "best places to work" recognition, and the business in Asia flourished and grew rapidly and profitably.

Managing director of Jones Lang LaSalle, Thailand, Suphin Mechuchep was recognized as one the most influential women in Thailand three years in a row. The current Asia Pacific CEO, Alastair Hughes, leveraged the momentum created by his predecessor and has continued to build and foster inclusive diversity and a multicultural mindset.

The transglobal leadership model inspires diversity on all fronts. We are quite optimistic that with the right focus and development, we will begin to see better progress in creating transglobal leaders. Andrés Tapia has written, "While it's important to address diversity issues within a country, we must also address them across countries."[25] Transglobal leaders are already moving in the right direction; others following in their footsteps can make this a game-changing and impactful movement.

- Coauthor Linda Sharkey, as vice president of people development and also responsible for leading diversity at Hewlett-Packard, reshaped the face of diversity for the company. She was able to take diversity global, and she worked with the CEO and senior leaders to appoint a global "diversity czar": Francisco Serrafini. Serrafini was the managing director for HP in the EMEA, and he was passionate about global diversity and the advancement of women. Together Linda and Serrafini created a transglobal inclusive steering committee to guide the efforts of the company. Serrafini and Linda's team built diversity into the talent processes of the company, and they held talent forums in each of the regions to identify the high-potential women as a means of making them visible to the senior leaders and hiring managers. Serrafini and his team regularly reviewed the talent and the open roles, and they actively worked to promote women up the organization ladder. During this time frame a substantial number of women were promoted, which sent a powerful message to the organization of inclusion and career advancement.

TRANSGLOBAL LEADERSHIP AND DIVERSITY TRENDS

As we saw above, the dimensions that distinguish our transglobal leaders from local leaders strongly relate to company performance through diversity strategies. Our transglobal leadership model is sustainable, and it constantly reminds us of the ephemeral nature of the business world and how things are continually in a state of flux. The following megatrends related to diversity are changing the complexion of the workforce and creating the need for a new form of transglobal leadership.

Generational Shifts

- Leaders are having to deal simultaneously with the idiosyncrasies of four generations: the silent generation, that is, people born between 1925 and 1945; the baby boomer generation; generation X, that is, people born between the early 1960s and the early 1980s; and generation Y.

- More members of generation Y (the "Google generation") are entering the ranks of leaders.

- Habits of different age groups are creating new forms of communication systems (Twitter, texting, and mobile device obsessions).

- The emerging workforce is demanding shifts in workplace practices (flexible schedules, telecommuting privileges).

- Today employers are dealing with four generations in the workplace, but by 2020 there will be five generations, and each will bring its own values and beliefs and a different lens to the workplace.[26]

Changing Racial and Ethnic Composition of the Workforce

- East and West continue to differ in their cultural habits and customs.

- Minority representation is changing; birthrates of people of color are high in the United States.[27]

- Growth in the numbers of African, Hispanic, and Asian Americans in the U.S. workforce will outpace that of Caucasians by a significant margin over the next 5 to 10 years.[28]

- Growth in the numbers of expats in most countries around the world will be at an all-time high.

Mobility on the Rise, Creating New Cultural Norms

- Short-term assignments and extended business travel are on the rise.[29]

- Future expatriate activity is expected to grow.[30]

- Assignee profiles will emphasize young, single employees.

- Assignee destinations will expand into emerging markets.[31]

- More companies will be seeking assessment tools to reduce the incidence of failed assignments.[32]

Rapid Growth of Brazil, Russia, India, China, (BRIC) and Other Countries; U.S. Dominance Being Challenged

- The third great power shift of the modern era is "the rise of the rest," reflecting rapid growth not only in the BRIC countries but also among others such as South Africa.[33]

- Economic growth should continue to accelerate in China, Germany, and India.

- China's gross domestic product (GDP) will likely outpace that of the United States, with dramatic implications for the world economy.

Gender Shifts

- More and more women will demand that the glass ceiling be shattered.

- Women senior executives such as Sheryl Sandberg, COO of Facebook, will be making impactful pleas to compel businesses to focus on the development and mentoring of high-potential, aspiring women.

- Research conducted by McKinsey, Catalyst, and others (discussed earlier in this chapter) will have an increasing influence on the thinking about how to close the gender gap.

Game-Changing Technology and Information Tsunami

- Social media networking will grow more potent as a form of corporate communication.

- The world will continue to get flatter and smaller, with more virtual paradigms.

- People will increase the number of their intimate connections through Facebook, LinkedIn, and other emerging technologies.

Transglobal Leaders' Reactions to Each of These Megatrends

As shown in Table 6.2, each of the five dimensions of transglobal leadership reflects how transglobal leaders connect and coalesce around diversity.

WOMEN AS TRANSGLOBAL LEADERS

Although leadership talent, skill shortages, and sweeping demographic shifts have provoked diversity and inclusion strategies in large U.S. corporations over the past 20 years, progress in closing the gender gap has been disappointingly slow, and it has almost halted at times. Although better understood by the United States and other Western nations, the positive impact that inclusive diversity can have on a company's bottom line has not yet been fully appreciated or respected by many countries. Initiatives taken in this area have not generated the outcomes expected and are slow in taking hold in many parts of the world, including the United States. For instance, the 2011 McKinsey *Women Matter* study revealed that it takes CEO commitment to bring about change and to maintain gender diversity ecosystems within corporations. Not all CEOs have signed on to this commitment.

In a 2011 commencement speech at Barnard University, Sheryl Sandberg, COO of Facebook, recounted sadly the lack of equality in the number of women in senior executive ranks: "In America, as in the entire developed world, we are equals under the law. But the promise of equality is not equality. As we sit here looking at this magnificent blue-robed class, we have to admit something that's sad but true: men run the world. Of 190 heads of state, 9 are women. Of all the parliaments around the world, 13 percent of those seats are held by women. Of corporate America top jobs, 15 percent are women—a number that has not moved at all in the past nine years." The Internet video of Sandberg's speech at the 2010 Technology, Education, Design (TED) conference received

Table 6.2 Transglobal Leadership Diversity Matrix

Leadership Dimension	Characteristic Behaviors	Bridging Generational Gaps	Embracing Racial and Ethnic Diversity	Fostering Gender Egalitarianism
Uncertainty Resilience: Building on Differences and Complexity	Reads and analyzes situations from multiple perspectives	Tolerates generational quirks; is indulgent of various age groups' behaviors; clarifies for understanding; does not get hung up on generational jargon	Is not daunted by cultural and ethnic variations; does not generalize or stereotype; cherishes cognitive and cultural differences	Accommodates work–life balance and family-friendly programs; has flexible work rules and arrangements; manages work, not time
Team Connectivity: Integrating Across Boundaries	Adjusts own style and activities to enhance performance of others	Skilled at working with multiple generations; seeks input from various age groups; consciously looks to build heterogeneous multigenerational work teams	Influences the collaboration of diverse global groups; is a silo buster and removes geographic and cultural boundaries by modeling boundary-less behavior	Promotes female networking and role models to advance women within the company
Pragmatic Flexibility: Adapting to Other Cultures	Adjusts personal values and adapts to local cultures	Makes concerted effort to learn or accommodate generational interests	Learns cultures through experience—that is, when in China learns to live like the Chinese; attempts to learns local language, is intrigued by and appreciates local customs, foods, habits; travels well	Recognizes positive impact of gender diversity on company performance; maintains a gender diverse staff

Perceptive Responsiveness: Acting on Intuition and Fact	Anticipates changing needs of customers and stakeholders	Finds ways to cultivate and nourish generational identity; seeks to understand what inspires and motivates individuals	Finds ways to cultivate and nourish ethnic and racial identities; seeks to understand what inspires and motivates individuals	Works hard at creating a gender balanced entity; sets gender-specific goals for hiring, promoting, retaining, and developing women
Talent Orientation: Achieving Through People	Personally cares for the development and engagement of all employees	Accelerates development of high-potential junior talent, while continuously challenging and rewarding the more senior, mature high-performing contributors	Values individuality; achieves breakthrough thinking through diverse teams	Ensures advancement and mentoring of women within company

650,000 hits in just six months. "For any of us in this room today," she stated, "let's start out by admitting we're lucky. We don't live in the world our mothers lived in, our grandmothers lived in, where career choices for women were so limited." More women than men graduate from college and graduate school and receive doctoral degrees. Yet, she went on, "women are not making it to the top."[34]

Again, as discussed earlier, studies have repeatedly shown that groups with more women in their executive ranks and boards tend to perform better. Research conducted by Anita Woolley and Thomas Malone (*Harvard Business Review*) looked at the collective intelligence of 192 teams composed of members aged 18 to 60, and they found that those with more women performed better than those with mostly men.[35] Catalyst has reported that Fortune 500 companies with three or more women on the board had a significant performance advantage—73 percent better return on sales and 112 percent better return on invested capital—over those with fewer women.[36]

In another study, beyond that referenced earlier, women made up only 12.5 percent of the FTSE 100 corporate boards, up from 9.4 percent in 2004.[37] A 2008 report by the Equality and Human Rights Commission suggested that at this rate of change, it would take more than 70 years to achieve gender balance in U.K. boardrooms.[38]

Our study of transglobal leaders nevertheless gives us hope and shines a light on the opportunity for a more balanced picture. As stated earlier, women are as capable as men of succeeding as transglobal leaders. Approximately one-third of our survey respondents were women, and the results indicated that the responses of the male and female leaders were about the same along most of the items. However, there were some gender-based differences. Our female respondents were more likely than their male counterparts to report that they do the following:

- Underestimate (rather than overestimate) their own capabilities

- Reward people in "customized" (rather than standardized) ways

- Use people and human resource development (rather than technology) as strategic levers

- Show confidence in people to the extent they share their values (as opposed to the extent they perform)

- Anticipate (rather than be surprised by) the things people do

- Show compassion even if it jeopardizes the task at hand (rather than stay detached and focus on accomplishing the task)

- Share feelings of uncertainty and vulnerability (as opposed to conveying an image of success and total confidence even when the path forward is unclear)

These differences suggest that there is more to learn around this topic given that most of these differences may give women an edge over men with respect to the dimensions discussed throughout this book.

Although our study focused on transglobal leaders, it is obvious that we can equally talk about several global companies that could be characterized as transglobal companies. These companies have genuinely begun to seek gender parity as reflected by their board and executive committee composition and by their leadership development practices. We now empirically know that women and men have an equal chance of succeeding—of being on equal footing in dealing with the challenges facing the globalized world.

We do not dispute that there are differences in male and female archetypes. Geert Hofstede's work on masculinity and femininity identifies key gender differences and the societal and cultural dimensions that reinforce them: "Male achievement reinforces masculine assertiveness and competition; female care reinforces feminine nurturance, a concern for relationships and for the living environment."[39] On the other hand, we believe that these differences, leveraged effectively, can give a company a competitive edge in the global marketplace.

TAKING SMALL, SIMPLE STEPS TO DRIVE INCLUSIVE DIVERSITY

A common thread that ran consistently through the thoughts and actions of the transglobal leaders we interviewed can be summarized in the following three qualities that contribute to achieving a diverse, creative workforce. These were:

- Curious about the world; observing differences and learning from others' experiences; creating culturally synergistic activities

- Bold and adventurous in trying out new ideas; embracing cognitive, cultural, and material change

- Compassionate and kind

CONCLUSION: THE FUTURE DEFINED

As more and more leaders begin to transcend into the new age of global diversity, the following signs will indicate they have arrived:

- Leaders will no longer rely just on quotas and goals to create and sustain a diverse work group.

- Their teams will be heterogeneous, all individuals will be encouraged to offer new ideas, and respect and engagement levels will be extraordinarily enhanced.

- An inclusive and constructive culture will be the norm, and people will be genuinely inspired to do their best work every day.

- All leaders will take on what has been in the past the role of chief diversity officer for their groups, and diversity will be embedded in the business and its core processes.

- All countries will recognize the power of and will be passionate about generating superior value to the business and to clients through diverse teams.

The point is that diversity is in every organization today. Just stand at the front door of your office, and see the diversity of the people who walk through it, whether they are employees, customers or potential customers, or shareholders or suppliers. This fact cannot be ignored.

Thus the important question is not whether the workforce is diverse; it is. The real question is whether you have the leadership that can maximize the power of that diversity to continue to innovate and grow. The quotas game is over! The new inclusive diversity phenomenon demands that you determine how to maximize the power of a workforce that is diverse in just about every way.

It's not only about how many women you've promoted. It's about whether you maximize the diversity of your organization at all levels and whether you realize who your great talent is no matter who they are or where in the world they live. Transglobal leaders get this phenomenon inherently. Organization structures will be challenged and changed to tap the diversity of thought across the globe and through the generations. In Part III, you will have the opportunity to reflect on and analyze your own organization's structure to see if you are organized in a way to maximize for global talent capability.

ASSESSING AND DEVELOPING YOUR TRANSGLOBAL LEADERSHIP CAPABILITIES

art III of this book is designed to help you assess how well your company and people are poised to do business globally and how much of a global mindset they really have. This part will help you look at the makeup of your company and assess where the weak points may be and what to do about them. We will help you assess your organization at the overall enterprise level and walk you through a series of questions designed to determine whether you have created an organization for maximum global power or you are marginalizing your ability to grow successfully as a global company. We will also help you analyze the teams that you have created and evaluate how globally versatile they are. Once you know where you stand, you can then take concrete action to move the needle on the global front.

Chapter 7 will assist you in looking at your organization at the enterprise and team levels, revealing steps that you can take to increase your global competitive advantage. Then we will help you look at your people and analyze how they stack up in terms of having a global mindset. We will look at the people perspective from a pipeline and leadership point of view and identify what you can do to spot and recruit talent that can play in the global environment.

Chapter 8 provides a clear road map for how to assess individuals within the organization. Again, you will have a clear snapshot of where your organization stands with respect to talent, which will help you develop a concise and actionable strategy and plan with the goal of building your global talent capability.

In Chapter 9 we revisit the abbreviated version of our survey that you took in Chapter 1. You can compare the results—whether you were describing yourself or considering someone else for a global role—against those of our sample. This tool will help you determine what you need to do to stretch your global muscle and become a global talent asset whether you are leading global teams, planning to branch out into emerging markets, aspiring to bigger global roles, or promoting or hiring someone for a global role at board, executive, management, or individual contributor levels. We will provide tips to enable you to get started on your personal journey toward becoming a transglobal leader no matter where you are today. We will highlight best practices based on our interviews, personal experiences in large global companies, and analysis of what some of the most globally successful companies are doing.

CHAPTER 7

Where Are You on the Map of Global Capability?

We're a relatively new company; however, we've grown fast and have customers and partners all over the world. We now have employees in many different geographies; we recently acquired a company that expands our geographic footprint, and we are likely in the next several years to expand even more globally. As we continue to grow, I need to ensure I develop a team that reflects the world in which we do business. It's important that the talent in the finance department can look up and see that they can make a difference and get ahead even if they are not at the headquarters. Ensuring my team thinks and acts globally not only sends a strong message to talent that we want to keep and also attract but also to our customers and partners that we are diverse in our thinking and can understand their issues from a global perspective. We were recently ranked no. 3 on Fortune's "World's Best Multinational Workplace" list, which is great recognition for our efforts.

—NICK NOVIELLO, CFO OF NETAPP

Noviello nicely sums up the issues that we will explore in this chapter. You cannot consider that yours is a truly global company just because you employ diverse talent. The question is: Do you have an organization structure that enables you to tap the globally diverse talent you have at all levels, or do you have a structure that inhibits global talent from getting ahead into roles of increasing influence and decision making? Are you a company that has all your global talent at lower levels while the major decision makers reflect a homogeneous perspective? Is your company still operating as if it were doing business 10 or 20 years ago in a very different world and business environment? The issue here is that if your leadership levels and organization structures do not promote mobility and global careers, you will lose talent, and you will most certainly lose the creativity this global talent can bring.

While the focus of this book is on leaders, we look at them in a different way in this chapter. We take the diversity question discussed in Chapter 6 to the next level and examine the structures that global companies have put in place to maximize their global strategies. It is widely stated by strategy gurus like Michael Porter that "strategy is followed by structure." What we see, however, is that there is often a disconnect between the strategy that a company is professing ("being a significant global player in their market") and the structures it has put in place. This is why we see this aspect of transglobal leadership worthy of its own chapter.

The power of this chapter is to help you find the nexus between your strategy, your structure, and your leadership talent. If you are operating in the global arena and plan to expand, you must take a look at the structure you have in place to capitalize on globalization and the right skill sets or behavioral dimensions of your leaders and talent. It is the combination of the structure you put in place, the individuals you put in these roles, and the skill sets they bring to those roles that makes for powerful, winning synergies. This is not a book about strategy, but rather about how to strategically and operationally build transglobal leaders. Part of building transglobal leaders is giving them opportunities to be promoted and exercise significant influence and decision-making power within the structure of the company. Let's get started.

ASSESSING YOUR CURRENT ORGANIZATION AT THE ENTERPRISE LEVEL

When thinking about a global world and how to best function in it, you must initially look at the makeup of your current company. The first step in understanding your ability to compete in the global arena is to understand your current organization and what it looks like from a leadership perspective on three levels:

- The enterprise level

- The business unit and functional team level

- The individual talent level

By looking at these three levels of your organization, you can get a pretty good idea as to whether you are a company with a local-centric mindset or a truly global business able to function anywhere in the world no matter where you are based.

At the enterprise level, you should be asking the following questions:

- What is the national makeup of your senior-most leaders?

- Where are decisions made in the organization?

- Where does the power reside?

- Who holds the expatriate positions?

- Is there a pipeline of global talent?

The answers to these questions will show how well you have structured your organization for global success and your ability to use your structure to develop transglobal leadership experience. They will also highlight your selection and hiring practices at the executive and next level down. Once you have done this analysis from a position, organization, and decision-making perspective, you can make a reasoned judgment about where you stand. Let's explore this more fully.

We all know that the top leadership of any organization shapes the context, the perspective, and the lens through which the business environment is viewed. Senior leadership also shapes the culture and norms of the company. If you want norms that promote and reinforce a global mindset, you must have leaders who value a global mindset. The first step in determining global capability is to take a serious look at the leadership of your organization at the top of the house. Using our global scale shown in Figure 7.1, plot your executive team to see how much of a diverse and global perspective these individuals offer. If all your executive team members are from the same geography, you would give your company a low score. If you have some transglobal leaders on the team, you might give your company a 5. If you have a good mix of transglobal leadership reflecting the depth of business, the extent of opportunity, and the major regions of the world in which you do business, you would put your company on the top end of the scale. If your leadership hails from one local mindset and your company falls on the

1	5	10
Local Only	Some Global Diversity	Strong Global Mix of Talent

Figure 7.1   Transglobal Executive Team Leadership Assessment

left side of the spectrum, this is a red flag in terms of your longer-term global functionality.

Take a look at the picture that this analysis paints. Are you a company that operates around the world but all your executive team members are from your home country? An executive team that looks and thinks homogeneously is one sure bet that the global mindset and openness to doing business differently in different parts of the world may be in short supply.

Royal Philips Electronics, based in the Netherlands, comes to mind here as an example of a company that could enhance its global mindset. While Philips is a successful company, it is not the top-tier player in many of the markets in which it competes. When you examine its executive team, you see that it is made up of a disproportionate number of executives who are from the Netherlands and also reside there. The company could be potentially even more successful in the global arena if it accelerates its global leadership development initiatives.

In comparison, Unilever's leadership team is reflective of the world in which it does business. It actively moves executives around the world to build broad global experience. It has a globally diverse executive team that brings to bear unique perspectives and nuances to its products and approaches to reflect cultural differences in local markets.

Another good example is Procter & Gamble. It is one of the most successful global companies and a dominant player in the sale of personal care and home items around the world, and—not coincidentally—it has an extremely global executive team.

A new entrant into the global marketplace is Huawei—the Chinese technology company. This company is actively recruiting talent from all over the world and ensuring that the talent reflects a truly global perspective. It is quickly becoming a powerhouse in the technology space. While at this point the company is dominated by Chinese nationals, the senior leaders are proactively working to increase the depth of transglobal leadership at the top of the house and doing a great job of attracting some key global players.

On the opposite side of the spectrum, two other companies come to mind in the global arena—Google and Facebook. Both are great companies, but they are decidedly United States centric. They are in their infancy from an organizational perspective, and they will no doubt be confronting some of these leadership and talent issues as they continue to grow. The GE executive team is somewhere in the middle. Its leadership team has begun to achieve global diversity, but it still has not completely cracked the U.S.-centric code. However, when you look at GE's company officers below the C-level, you see a great global mix of talent. This is the result of a conscious effort on the part of GE leaders to ensure that they reflect in their leadership the perspective of the regions of the world in which they do business. Disney, which had early challenges in moving into global markets, has actively worked to increase its global representation in its leadership and board.

Using the scale shown in Figure 7.2, let's do the same exercise for your organization's board. Take a good look at who holds your board seats. Is the board bringing the global perspective that the company needs to function in multiple and diverse cultures?

Now let's look at the leadership makeup of the senior executive roles below the executive team. Who holds the top leadership roles reporting to the C-suite? Again, use Figure 7.2 as a scale for your assessment.

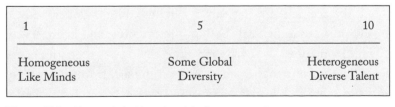

1	5	10
Homogeneous Like Minds	Some Global Diversity	Heterogeneous Diverse Talent

Figure 7.2 Transglobal Leadership Assessment

In some companies, you look around and see like minds, and in others like GE, you see a conscious effort to rotate and mix leaders from around the world to bring in new thinking and global perspectives and to stretch talent. GE invests a lot of time and effort to expose leadership talent to other parts of the globe and the local operations there. A cautionary note here is that if companies see their leaders as being diverse in only the classic sense of ethnicity, they may mistakenly think they have a global perspective. However, the classic sense of diversity and true transglobal diversity are two entirely different things, as we pointed out in Chapter 6. If the power positions in a company are held by individuals who, by and large, are from the same country culture regardless of ethnicity and similar characteristics, they will still hold the norms and views emanating from that culture. We want to be cautious here on another front: just because people are from one culture, it does not mean they can't be highly effective transglobal leaders. Our research has shown that they can be if they exhibit the characteristics of a transglobal leader that are discussed in Chapter 5. Nevertheless, the point is that if your company is widely homogeneous at its leadership core, this is at least one significant factor to prompt you to look deeper into your organization and develop a concerted strategy to expand the global mix.

The next question to ask is: Where are the predominant decisions made? Are they made in the power center of the company, or is decision making dispersed to key parts of the globe where they can take into account local markets and cultures? Use the scale shown in Figure 7.3 to rate your company.

If the decision-making power is in one country alone and held by like-minded individuals both at the executive and board levels, trouble looms ahead. We have recounted numerous examples of the financial disasters that resulted, at least in part, from this type of makeup and decision-making process. In the U.S. auto industry, for example, an assumption that the industry leaders made years ago is that the world would adopt the American vision of the large, gas-

1	5	10
All Made at Epicenter	Some Field Authority	Dispersed Throughout Appropriately

Figure 7.3 Decision-Making Assessment

guzzling automobile regardless of local constraints. American auto-makers have since learned that people in other countries will not buy those large cars and have built many new vehicles, including smaller cars and hybrids, that reflect consumers' needs in local markets.

If you have worked in large global companies, you know that a critical issue to be solved is where decisions are made. In just about every region—whether it is the Europe, Middle East, and Africa (EMEA) region, the Asia Pacific region, or the Americas—if all decisions go to the top of the house in one place, it reduces the speed at which the company can do business. Such centralized decision making causes regional leaders to take inordinate amounts of time creating pitches and convincing the senior leaders to move forward in time to beat the local or regional competition.

Genpact, the global outsourcing powerhouse, is a company that hails from India but has been able to secure a good balance on the leadership team. While many are from or have roots in India, most have spent substantial amounts of time working and living in other parts of the globe. Genpact is arguably one of the best out-sourcing companies in the world and has a blue-chip list of clients.

"Tiger" Tyagarajan, the president and CEO of Genpact, reorganized his company to shift the "center of gravity" of his leadership team to be closer to the customer and did away with a formal headquarters. According to Tiger, a longtime organization innovator, "Having no formal headquarters allows us to make decisions that affect our customers quicker and provides us the speed and flexibility to grow our business. Innovation always happens in every industry when leaders are close to their customers, they collaborate and co-innovate and pick up signals on what changes are coming. They are then able to drive change through their organization with speed. Speed, flexibility, and innovation are key to our success, in fact to the long-term success of any company in every industry. Having a distributed leadership model leveraging the technology available today means we as leaders have to have a great deal of trust, a very clear strategy that we all embrace, and one set of underlying leadership behaviors and values that are clearly defined and understood and lived by all of us." Genpact has moved quickly into the outsourcing space and has leadership dispersed throughout the globe.

Richard Solomons, CEO of IHG, further makes the point about the importance of dispersed decision making. "One of IHG's guiding principles is 'Freedom within a framework,' and we give clarity about certain things, that is, the core basis of the global brand, but we give freedom to adapt this locally. You cannot succeed as a global hotelier if you have rigid environments. It is far easier to deal with ambiguity if you have a framework . . . a starting point from which you can argue to modify. We have base standards that we hope everyone understands, but they also understand they can be modified from the base, given local conditions."

The next piece to examine at the enterprise level is where the senior leadership positions are located in the company. Are your directors or division heads and above located in your home country, or are they dispersed throughout the world? Is there an inordinate amount of promotional positions at headquarters, or can talent have reasonable career progression to senior roles of influence if they are not at that location? Obviously, certain senior roles will exist only at the headquarters level, but is your organization structured in such a way that great global talent is precluded from advancing? Because great talent always seeks stretch assignments and promotional opportunities, they may leave your organization for advancement elsewhere.

In an analysis by Hewlett-Packard of the senior positions in the company, it was clear that advancement was largely in the United States, particularly in Palo Alto, California, at the company's headquarters. Getting great talent in other regions at the midcareer level was tough for a number of reasons, but at least one contributing factor was that talent could not realize career progression unless they moved to the headquarters. A top succession internal candidate was lost because the company insisted that the candidate reside in the United States for what was arguably a worldwide role. This person is now the CEO of a very successful company in Europe. To HP's credit, its senior leaders, once they understood the issue, did a great deal to balance the leadership roles across the globe, and they now have a strong cadre of successful transglobal leaders.

A great example of a company that has moved beyond boundaries and headquarters is Jones Lang LaSalle. It does not really have a headquarters, per se, but rather, it operates with an executive committee and board that reflect the world. It holds its executive committee meetings in various locations, and it is not bound to any particular country in terms of how and where it functions. Of the top 8 executive roles, 3 are American, 2 Scottish, 1 English, 1 Indian, and 1 German. The 11-member board is similarly diverse (4 English, 5 Americans, 1 Belgian, and 1 Chinese); 4 of the members are women, including the chair, and many achieved their formal qualifications in countries other than their home country.

The final issue to watch out for at the enterprise level is on the expatriate front. Take a good look at the profiles of your leaders who hold expatriate roles. Are they all from the same country, or do they reflect the global nature of your business? Have you identified a cadre of leaders who are capable of moving anywhere in the world and growing the business regardless of where their passports were issued? If your analysis indicates that you mostly have home-country talent from the epicenter on expatriate assignments, this is another red flag that could indicate you are not developing your talent equally around the world so that you can compete most effectively in the global arena.

Summary of the Enterprise Review

When you are looking at your enterprise, make sure that you are structured for success. Ask the following questions, and be honest with your answers:

- Do the senior executives reflect the global nature of the business?

- Do the members of the board reflect the global nature of the business?

- Is decision making dispersed to key areas of the globe and power balanced for fast insight, decision making, and execution?

- Are the senior leadership roles a good reflection of the global markets in which you do business?

- Do the expatriates reflect a cross section of the countries in which you operate?

On a scale of 1 to 10, does your organization score in the top range on the above questions? If not, your company has some work to do to ensure that it is a globally focused organization and not trapped with a singular lens that is keeping globally dexterous talent from succeeding and moving ahead.

ASSESSING YOUR CURRENT ORGANIZATION AT THE BUSINESS UNIT AND FUNCTIONAL TEAM LEVEL

Assessing talent in the business units and the functional areas can reveal a lot about the global mindset of the company and its leaders. The same questions asked above can also be asked about the respective business units and how they function in your organization. You may be a highly global company, but you may have pockets or business units that fall into the local-perspective trap and don't embrace global thinking in the people they hire, promote, and move into expatriate roles. It is not enough to just look across the enterprise. It is also necessary to take a deeper look. Each business and functional unit should do the same analysis and move to take corrective action to be truly global. If the analysis of the top of the house indicates that senior leaders are in the middle or bottom quartile of having global talent and a global mindset, it will be difficult, but not impossible, to initiate changes at the business unit and functional team level.

At the functional level, this need for a global perspective can be completely overlooked (frequently, in a misguided attempt to save money) in the rush for centers of excellence. Examining functions and understanding their global mindset can make all the difference between having a marketing campaign that is just good or fails completely and one that is great. There have been many missteps in naming products that don't reflect global nuances. Well-publicized examples from the 2010 Olympics in China highlighted that services were named in such a way that they were not effectively understood by Olympians from all over the world.

While it may not be feasible to have globally diverse functional teams, companies certainly need functional teams with global experience. Functional teams that do not understand the business challenges in each locale in which they operate cannot be good advisors to the business and help leaders make reasoned decisions around tax, legal, marketing, hiring, and intellectual property issues. Functional leaders and business leaders must rely heavily on the perceptive responsiveness and pragmatic flexibility dimensions to design and support programs that can play anywhere in the world. We offer the matrix shown in Figure 7.4 for analyzing where your business unit and functional team talent is relative to global acumen.

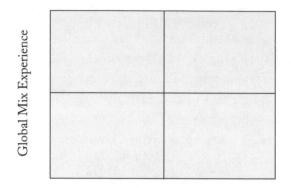

Business Mix Experience

Figure 7.4   Global Acumen Matrix

Plot your functional teams into the matrix, and see what the picture tells you. This information can give you a clear road map for what you may need to change to compete more effectively on the global level. It can also help illuminate if you have business units that operate in silos where promotions and career paths are strictly within the function and there is little inclusion of others from different types of businesses, models, or geographies.

We are reminded of a story about an American attorney who was sent to Asia on an expatriate assignment. When he got there, he had a great deal to learn about the complex legal environment of the Asian markets. There was a local attorney who had practiced in the region for years who was ready for a promotion. He was passed over for the American expatriate. Regional business leaders scratched their heads as to why this American was hired from outside the company for the role. The credibility of the hiring manager of the American expatriate was clearly challenged, and his motive was suspected as being biased. The message that the hire sent to regional leaders was very telling. The skilled attorney ready for a promotion ultimately left the company for a competitor. The American lawyer had to supplement his limited local knowledge with external and expensive legal advice in a number of local jurisdictions.

SUMMARY OF THE BUSINESS UNIT AND FUNCTIONAL TEAM REVIEW

The above analysis also enables you to see where you have talent in different functions that are ready for bigger global roles. This should help determine whether the organization has a good pipeline of global talent ready for growth roles. Are you poised to fully maximize your business in an increasingly global world?

ASSESSING YOUR CURRENT ORGANIZATION AT THE INDIVIDUAL TALENT LEVEL

At this level, you are examining the individual talent of the organization. Many of the steps outlined above should be included in your yearly overall review of talent. Most companies review talent only to determine succession and potential for further development, frequently failing to utilize the lens of global capability in their assessment. Here are some questions that you should be thinking about to ensure that you have a global talent powerhouse:

- Is there a pipeline of top talent in the major countries in which you do business?

- Is there a development plan for the talent that stretches their global acumen?

- What is the ratio of global to local top talent in the talent pool?

- What is the attrition rate of global talent, and where in the organization is it occurring? For example, a country, level, function, or region?

- How well is global talent accepted into the organization if they are hired from the outside?

- Do you have "blockers" who are creating a ceiling for global talent promotion?

- Do you invest sufficient time and money in developing talent from around the world?

- Are your training initiatives designed to develop top talent balanced and inclusive of global candidates?

- Do you have global talent in your succession plans, and do you use these plans to fill open positions?

Four companies that spend a great deal of time on the individual talent level are Procter & Gamble, Jones Lang LaSalle, Hewlett-Packard, and General Electric. GE, in particular, put the global lens into its talent review process many years ago, and it has borne fruit for the company, and GE now has a cadre of leaders who hail from multiple geographies and have lived in many places outside their home-country borders. P&G also operates this way. HP and Jones Lang LaSalle largely use expatriate assignments as development opportunities. It is not uncommon for these companies to scout and recruit talent in emerging markets and put them into leadership development initiatives that are a combination of classroom learning and global assignments. They invest heavily in moving talent into stretch roles both from a business perspective and a geographic perspective. Since these companies have been growing global talent for a long time, they have a senior talent pool that can deploy anywhere and successfully build the business. These companies have one overarching value in common: developing people. Transglobal leaders are expected to identify local talent and grow and develop that talent to succeed them. In fact, their ability to grow local talent is used as one measure of their success.

Succession planning is also a very telling factor to look at when determining the global mindset. Jones Lang LaSalle does a particularly good job of ensuring that its top-level succession plans are global and that leadership talent is moved around the world into increasing positions of influence. This company has senior succession plans for existing leaders ready for bigger assignments, as well as deep succession plans that look several layers down and begin to move talent into new roles early in their careers. The result of this type of succession planning is that Jones Lang LaSalle has limited loss from within its global talent pool, and it is always ready with options when the time comes to fill senior positions. Over the last five years, the percentage annual loss of global talent within the 200 leaders identified and nurtured is less than 3 percent.

While we believe that many organizations use some type of yearly talent review, putting a sharp global lens on the discussion and analysis can be very revealing in terms of how poised they are today to compete. More important, how well they are developing the talent necessary to compete tomorrow in this rapidly globalizing world.

BUILDING AN ACTION PLAN FOR CHANGE

Here are some actions that your organization can take to increase its global acumen and transglobal leadership. For example, an analysis can uncover a certain element of bias that may exist in your organization—a level of bias that is obvious to others but not to you. After you have conducted a careful analysis, you then need to build a plan for change, with the makeup of that plan being based on where you are in the organization. If you lead the enterprise, your actions should focus on building a structure that represents the global nature of the company:

- Actively recruit board and executive committee members with global backgrounds.

- Ensure that you have vetted board and executive committee members for the essential characteristics of transglobal leaders (as discussed in Chapter 5 and addressed further in Chapter 8).

- Do the same for the leadership team that reports to you. Look at the people in the pipeline who could be successors for your current executives, and make plans to get them ready for those roles.

- Ensure that the leaders at the next level are accountable for conducting an organizational assessment of their global capability and that they are taking appropriate action.

- Build global talent discussions into your overall talent strategy for the company.

- Develop a cadre of top talent who can go anywhere in the world to build the business—make them the exemplars of the leadership model for senior roles.

- Start building functional global pipelines now, before you actually need to expand in a market and find you don't have the talent to do so.

- When the company is working on cross-border mergers and acquisitions, make sure you have a pool of functional and line executives who possess a good level of the five global dimensions we have highlighted. This includes the initial evaluation team, the due diligence team, and the integration team.

Conducting the analysis above is really a first step in getting a snapshot of your organization's global capability. This analysis will also identify the company's "hot spots" and where you need to take action to even out the organization and build balanced views of conducting business in the global arena. One caution here: after you complete this analysis and determine that you do have globally focused talent with global experience, do not assume that they have the essential personal characteristics to be transglobal leaders. The analysis will not tell you which leaders have the ability to really leapfrog the competition globally. These characteristics can be understood only by determining the behavioral dimensions of your current leaders, future leaders, and those you hire.

Here is a perfect example: The executive committee of a large publicly traded company was struggling to find offshore talent. Its members did not believe that anyone outside their company's own sphere would properly understand the business. This executive committee believed that it understood global cultures and perspectives because it had two people not born in the United States in its ranks. However, one was an Indian who had not lived in India or worked outside the United States for 30 years, and the other was a South American who had not lived on that continent for 20 years. This did not make for a global executive team!

CONCLUSION

To truly be successful on a global level, a clear understanding of the skill strengths and gaps among your leaders is needed. Reviewing how your organization is structured today and where you need to make changes combined with reviewing the current global skills of your talent will paint a powerful picture for action. Without this combined analysis, it will be difficult to:

- Understand the magnitude of the change required.

- Recognize the degree of bias that exists in your system and the extent to which it prevents you from dealing with complex global issues.

- Understand the skills and training that need to be developed to have globally savvy leaders.

- Drive development actions that will move the organization forward to have truly transglobal leaders.

- Require that each leader promoted to a bigger global role has been assessed against the essential characteristics of a transglobal leader and has a personal action plan to continue to grow global muscle.

Chapter 8 will go into detail on how to assess and develop transglobal leaders using a three-pronged approach: What do you look for in early talent? How do you assess and nurture the midtier of your organization? And, how do you ensure that you have senior leaders who are fully skilled for the global world?

Developing Global Capability

*The first time I went abroad (to France) I was 12.
I found myself interested in languages, cultures,
and a desire to understand and be understood in the
different cultures and the countries I lived in or visited.
The challenge is the need to be different in different
countries—such as China, Brazil, and Germany—to
understand what makes the people tick, to listen and
to adapt to people's interests. It's not about you or your
country; you cannot simply relate or draw from your
national roots or your personal frame of reference. Today,
as CEO, I have to be a Federalist, and I have to pull
people together, so they feel part of the whole. People
are not bound by assets but by the desire to work. In a
federation, people want to dial into the whole, given
freedom and respect.*

—COLIN DYER, CEO OF JONES LANG LASALLE

Acquiring, developing, and retaining global talent is a top priority for CEOs looking to grow their business, particularly to expand into nascent global markets where skilled talent is hard to find. It is predicted that transglobal leadership skills will continue to be in crucial demand, making both acquisition and retention of global talent a challenge for business leaders and human resources professionals. Conventional programs might work by accident, but they are not likely to consistently deliver the talent that is needed to build and sustain global capability.

Transglobal leaders generate positive energy from listening to and learning from people around them and leveraging differences. We heard time and time again from many of our successful transglobal leaders that they had early experiences that shaped and cultivated their transglobal skills. Some had opportunities very early in life, even before they reached the age of 20, to live in a multicultural environment and to learn from people of various ethnic and cultural backgrounds. Leaders who play on a global stage or get moved away from home tend to have experienced being an ethnic minority very early in their career. Some of the leaders in our sample lived overseas as children or had parents who were in the military or foreign service or were expats. They were able to gain experience adapting to unfamiliar cultures and surroundings early in their lives.

We also found transglobal leaders who did not have these early experiences to shape their leadership style but nevertheless were highly successful in a global setting and strongly displayed the dimensions described in Chapters 4 and 5. As we started to delve a bit deeper into this group, we found that these individuals in their early years tended to explore new and varied things. They introduced multicultural experiences into their day-to-day activities by reading diverse literature, enjoying music of various genres, attempting to learn different languages, or seeking a deeper learning of history, arts, and sciences. They were doggedly curious about the world, and they expanded their horizons intellectually to make up for missed opportunities of experiential learning. As they journeyed through their world of literature, history, and the arts, their personalities and identities were shaped and influenced by the diversity of their learning.

How do we focus the spotlight on these individuals and find them in our search for global talent? How do we begin to recognize the foundational behaviors and attitudes earlier in careers and develop the talent for advanced global responsibilities?

A simple four-pronged approach will jump-start the process and speed up the development at various levels and stages of the leader's growth (see Figure 8.1). These stages are not sequen-

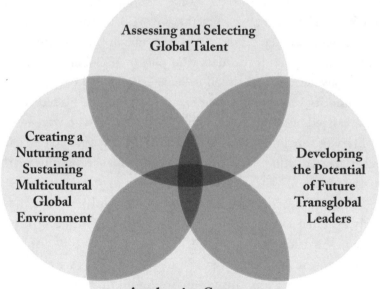

Figure 8.1 A Four-Pronged Approach to Developing Global Capability

tial, but they need to be customized based on the point in time of an individual's career. The most important part of this process is detecting the talent and recognizing someone's aptitude to be a transglobal leader. Our study revealed that not everyone is suitable for or would derive satisfaction from a global role. Certain elements of the five dimensions can be learned and developed, while others may be somewhat difficult to introduce once individuals become set in their ways as local leaders.

ASSESSING AND SELECTING GLOBAL TALENT

How does one spot talent when recruiting in different countries? How does one recognize whether an individual will have a difficult time adjusting in another city within their own country, let alone a country overseas? We'll address these questions by beginning with the stories of two people who were raised quite differently but emerged as successful leaders managing global teams in several countries. Both worked for the same company.

Alastair Hughes, who is Scottish-born and on the surface may appear parochially Scottish, has been successfully leading a Jones Lang LaSalle region of 14 countries in the Asia Pacific (AP) for the past two and a half years. During his tenure, the revenue and profits within the region have grown substantially. One might argue that the Asia Pacific region is the land of opportunity and emerging markets are growing rapidly; however, prior to being appointed head of the AP, he ran the Europe, Middle East, and Africa (EMEA) region for three years, leading 17 countries through an equally successful period of unprecedented expansion, double-digit growth, and profitability.

Hughes epitomizes the "transglobal" in our model. He spent the very early years of his life in Edinburgh in a very homogeneous setting until his parents moved to Kuwait, where he spent the majority of his adolescent years in a multicultural setting. He attended a coeducational school where his classmates were of nationalities from every conceivable part of the world, and he grew up appreciating their differences. He claims he is truly "color blind," and he really enjoys the diversity of people. His family moved back to London, where he went to college and then launched his career in real estate. Hughes moved up the corporate ladder with incredible speed, expanding his geographic footprint across London, France, Germany, the Middle East, Russia, China, India, and Australia. He is interested in people's personal stories of toil and success, which he believes enrich his own experience and make him a far better leader in a culturally diverse and highly complex organization.

In contrast to Hughes, coauthor Nazneen Razi, who was previously global head of HR at Jones Lang LaSalle, had never left her home country until she was 22 years old, when she emigrated from India to the United States. She had lived a rather sheltered life, yet one filled with rich learnings from her studies of world literature, the arts, history, and politics. Although most of the information was not experiential, when combined with her passion and desire to experience real life and when given the opportunity, she emerged as a highly successful individual in mostly global executive assignments that took her to places and geographies in various parts of the world. Her career also spanned multiple industries such as insurance, technology, education, and real estate, providing her a broad spectrum of experiences across geographies, industries, and cultures.

So what sort of questions does one ask these two successful transglobal leaders? How does one discover their potential to lead anywhere in the world? We have found that to unlock the secrets of individuals' potential and better gauge their aptitude, we have to probe in the areas of the five behavioral dimensions and ask them to reflect on their formative years, describing their early activities, experiences, and environment.

We have found that the mere assessment of cognitive abilities using standard interview protocols is not adequate to draw out the cultural, emotional, and moral nuances and propensities in an individual. When considering junior talent for a global role, we suggest employing the simple interview protocol in Table 8.1. We recognize that structured interviews are not always the most effective, but they are a start. Additional indicators of the individuals' performance and their global and cultural sensitivities can be uncovered and validated over time. The interview protocol is one of the tools that can help distinguish transglobal leaders from local leaders, particularly in combination with other tools described in this book. A study of the practical application of the five transglobal leadership dimensions to real-world problem solving could be used to help reveal the potential for success in junior talent.

Table 8.1   Transglobal Leadership Interview Protocol

Questions	What This Probes For	Red Flags
1. Describe your interests and hobbies. What do you enjoy most outside of work?	Diversity in learning and preference for team versus individual activities	Preference for non-team sports and events; lack of passion for extracurricular activities
2. Do you discuss your interests and hobbies with others? Provide examples of how you have learned from such sharing.	Desire to socialize, share, and learn from a wide variety of people	Overly reserved behavior; difficulty adjusting to or learning from others
3. Provide an example of when you modified your view of the world as a result of new and different information or opinions.	Willingness to flex opinions based on information from others	See the world mainly in their unique way
4. Do you find yourself following a schedule, or do you alter your course as you go along?	Ability to deal with change and uncertainty	Rigid, structured, or linear behavior and thinking

(continued on next page)

Table 8.1 Transglobal Leadership Interview Protocol *(continued)*

Questions	What This Probes For	Red Flags
5. Do you base your decisions and priorities on long-term strategy or on short-term demands and issues?	Willingness to invest in the future, while keeping short-term goals in check	Propensity to micromanage; tactical approach to work
6. Do you prefer projects and are more satisfied with long-term results or those that are quick hits and produce instant results?	Future orientation; willingness to delay short-term gratification to achieve long-term gains	Present orientation; want immediate gratification
7. What types of books and other reading materials do you enjoy the most?	Depth and breadth of interests and knowledge; openness to reading materials that transcend cultural boundaries	Mainly focused on a singular genre or type of reading materials
8. Do you learn mostly from books and the Internet or from people? Do you enjoy healthy debates on issues and topics?	Type of learning and learning style	Dogmatic approach to learning; getting information mostly from impersonal sources
9. What types of travel do you enjoy most? What destinations have given you the most satisfaction or sense of fulfillment?	Interest in people and places of historical, political, and cultural interest	Lack of interest in other cultures; mostly vacation for relaxation versus learning; staying in the hotel rather than mingling with locals
10. Describe how you learn from and adapt to new surroundings.	Adaptability and flexibility	Difficulty moving out of their comfort zone
11. Provide examples of when you have promoted solutions, products, or services that transcend geographical boundaries.	Interest in cross-geographical and cross-cultural ideas and concepts	Higher preoccupation in local markets

Table 8.1 Transglobal Leadership Interview Protocol *(continued)*

Questions	What This Probes For	Red Flags
12. Describe a situation in which you had to make adjustments to your thinking or communication style as a result of cultural or other differences of your audience.	Perceptive enough to change their way of thinking and behaving in response to situations or people outside their normal frame of reference	Uncompromising; emphasis on personal beliefs and standards and not open to those of others
13. Describe the composition of the teams you select or how you select your team members.	Priority on diversity in creating teams and seeking out global talent	Lack of global diversity in team composition
14. As a child, did you travel outside your home country? At what age did you first experience another culture? Did you do other things to learn about people in other countries?	Cross-cultural experiences or curiosity; exposure to diverse groups during formative years	Lack of interest or knowledge about other cultures
15. Do you bend rules and values as required by the situation, or do you refuse to compromise on principles (even if they conflict with local norms)?	Moral intelligence; examples demonstrate if "bending" the rules constitutes flexibility or crosses the line	Reluctance to bend rules even when situation may warrant an exception; respond more favorably to rules and rigid behaviors
16. How do you as well as other people evaluate your success?	Focus of evaluation: individual versus team performance	Imbalance in team versus individual, with individual performance being the dominating influence
17. If you could invite anyone to a dinner party, whom would you invite?	Value differences and cultural or global diversity	Prefer people with similar backgrounds and experiences
18. How do you reward people for performing well?	Use of customized rewards	Insensitivity to people's personal needs and values in providing reinforcement

DEVELOPING THE POTENTIAL
OF FUTURE TRANSGLOBAL LEADERS

Once you have identified leaders who have the potential to succeed in a multicultural environment, how do you develop them so their potential is revealed, unlocked, and maximized in the global arena? As a refresher, we would like to revisit some of the descriptors of the five dimensions of behaviors that are characteristic of transglobal leaders. These are the characteristics on which you should focus as you mine for global talent and develop your teams.

Uncertainty Resilience: Building on Differences and Complexity

- They use out-of-the-box thinking.

- They can make decisions in situations where things are not crystal clear.

- They are confident when addressing complex problems.

- They seek out and handle change and complexity with ease.

- They are bored by or dislike the status quo.

- They have a negative reaction to linear, overly detailed analysis.

- They stress strategic vision, opportunities, and goals.

Team Connectivity: Integrating Across Boundaries

- They adjust activities to enhance the performance of others.

- They take responsibility when things go wrong.

- They collaborate with and support their teams and are sensitive to "what's in it for the team."

- They are not likely to act selfishly or at others' expense.

- They come across as "doing the right thing" by others.

- They act based on the needs of others and the organization.

- They are oriented toward personal and team mastery and adaptation.

- They respond negatively to egoism.

Pragmatic Flexibility: Adapting to Other Cultures

- They adjust their personal values to get the job done.

- They emphasize the needs of the work group.

- They develop higher-order and win-win solutions.

- They are not likely to dismiss others' views by being unyielding.

- They are tolerant.

- They adjust to different approaches, perspectives, and situations.

- They are oriented toward consensus and action.

- They are willing to compromise if a situation warrants it.

Perceptive Responsiveness: Acting on Intuition and Fact

- They anticipate the changing needs of customers.

- They use negative feedback as an impetus for change and development.

- They encourage overarching frameworks that allow for diversity.

- They move to be customer centric.

- They reject one-size-fits-all approaches.

- They come across as astute and discerning.

- They create meaning out of ambiguity through a combination of intuition and information.

- They treat people as individuals.

Talent Orientation: Achieving Through People

- They personally engage in talent development rather than relying on HR to manage talent and succession.

- They get involved with and drive succession planning initiatives.

- They emphasize the connection between people and organizational performance.

- They come across as being people oriented.

- They achieve effectiveness through people.

- They constantly tap human potential.

The matrix in Table 8.2 is useful in understanding which characteristics within each of these dimensions are easy to change and develop and which ones are more challenging and complex. On balance, it is easier to assess and alter behaviors and rather more difficult to change underlying assumptions and values. As behaviors change over time, they can influence assumptions and bring about gradual change in values and principles; however, that takes determination, effort, and conviction, as well as a commitment to make the change. When applying the matrix, keep in mind that when you change characteristics in columns 1 and 2, it is easier to change those in column 3.

Table 8.2 Ease of Changing Behaviors, Attitudes, and Beliefs Associated with the Five Dimensions of Transglobal Leaders

	Fairly Simple and Straightforward; Easy to Develop	More Involved; Requires More Intricate and Dedicated Development Efforts	Challenging; May Be More Difficult to Develop or Change
Uncertainty Resilience: Building on Differences and Complexity	Consciously hiring diverse teams Creating an environment where people are allowed to learn from mistakes	Making decisions in a situation in which not everything is crystal clear Addressing complex problems with confidence Seeking and handling change and complexity with ease Stressing strategic vision, opportunities, goals Thinking out of the box	Deep-seated resistance to change and a strong predisposition to homogeneity Predisposition to rigidity
Team Connectivity: Integrating Across Boundaries	Collaborating and supporting the team Taking responsibility when things go wrong	Adjusting activities to enhance the performance of others Coming across as doing the right thing Acting based on the needs of others and the organization Displaying orientation toward personal mastery and adaptation	Strong narcissistic tendencies Moving from Theory X to Theory Y, especially when Theory X assumptions of coercion and control are deeply engrained

(continued on next page)

Table 8.2 Ease of Changing Behaviors, Attitudes, and Beliefs Associated with the Five Dimensions of Transglobal Leaders *(continued)*

	Fairly Simple and Straightforward; Easy to Develop	More Involved; Requires More Intricate and Dedicated Development Efforts	Challenging; May Be More Difficult to Develop or Change
Pragmatic Flexibility: Adapting to Other Cultures	Emphasizing the needs of work group Making constructive compromises	Driving high-order solutions Adjusting to different approaches, perspectives, situations Focusing on consensus and action Compromising if situation warrants	Adjusting entrenched personal values in order to get to a higher order of collaboration Knowing when to compromise and when not to
Perceptive Responsiveness: Acting on Intuition and Fact	Encouraging overarching frameworks that allow for diversity Creating meaning out of ambiguity	Anticipating the changing needs of customers Minimizing the use of one-size-fits-all approaches Treating people as individuals	Coming across as astute, discerning, and sensitive Believing that people can be rewarded in different ways without being unfair
Talent Orientation: Achieving Through People	Personally engaging in talent development rather than relying on HR to manage talent and succession Getting involved and driving succession planning initiatives	Emphasizing the connection between people and organizational performance Tapping human potential; making sure enough time (ideally more than 30%) is spent on people responsibilities	Genuinely valuing people Developing a high level of trust

How to Develop the Five Transglobal Leadership Dimensions

In *Developing Global Executives*, McCall and Hollenbeck claim that the "good news" from their study is that the basic process for development is the same for all executives, regardless of the countries they come from or whether the development is for global, expatriate, or global executive work.[1] They acknowledge that the specifics applied to developing global rather than local executives are different in very significant ways and that the process is far more complex and unpredictable and requires greater focus.

Our study confirmed this complexity and revealed that experiential learning is the most powerful and impactful factor in developing the necessary global capabilities. Companies that benefit the most in building their global talent pipeline are those that offer international assignments and cross-cultural exchange opportunities to their high-potential employees. The earlier these experiences are allowed to take hold in one's career, the longer lasting and more accelerated the development. To build a global talent pool, companies must provide short- as well as long-term expatriate assignments, job swaps, and long-duration travel assignments that allow executives to spend meaningful time in unfamiliar countries and cultures. Equally critical is that these individuals take ownership of their development, entrench themselves in their new surroundings, and learn from the cultural differences and the diversity that are offered on the ground.

CASE STUDY

How to Make the Most of Your Cultural Experience— Adapting to Cultures and Being a Cultural Chameleon

Alastair Hughes, who has led in both the EMEA and Asia Pacific regions and has managed over 20,000 employees in over 30 countries, travels in excess of 50 percent of his time. He believes strongly that you need to "push away preconceptions, and one way of doing that is to get the local people comfortable so that they're not telling you what they think you want to hear but what is really meaningful to them."

It is important, he says, to choose your battles carefully and allow local interpretation of any regional or corporate strategy. "Cultural variations need to be considered when executing a strategy. Some cultures are very compliant and respectful of authority and will do as told, while others are recalcitrant cultures where an autocratic style will provoke defiance and lack of cooperation. You need to understand these behaviors and adapt your style. To understand the nuances of the various cultures, you must spend time immersing yourself into the social and work system. You cannot go to a country for a day on a 'presidential visit'; you need to get under the skin of the business."

When Hughes visits a country, he bans PowerPoint presentations. Instead he spends his time having more casual conversations with the leaders and staff. He prefers open, candid, nonscripted conversations that can produce more insight and learnings than any canned presentation.

Several leaders we interviewed shared stories similar to Alastair Hughes's in the case study. When traveling to a country, most leaders will prepare well in advance and will benefit from learning opportunities offered by their organizations. One of the companies that has done a good job enabling its leaders to survive, thrive, and flourish successfully in a global environment is Deloitte LLP. It has a very strong global deployment program that provides employees an opportunity to experience a work environment in a country outside their own. Leaders at Deloitte find themselves very well equipped to handle the challenges of leading in a complex environment. The case study in the sidebar describes a successful leader at Deloitte LLP and her personal stories and experiences working outside of the United States.

How to Prepare for a Cultural Experience

Another example of a leader who prepares for working in new cultures is Deborah DeHaas, vice chairman and central region managing partner for Deloitte LLP. Deb states, "Before I go to any new market, I seek to learn and understand the current environment, the political and social scene, the unique economic or market conditions, and any other factors impacting our client or our business. I also work hard at understanding the local culture by contacting the local leaders in advance and spending time in the local Deloitte Touche Tohmatsu limited member firm office before going to visit the client."

DeHaas also spends time outside work hours socializing with the local teams "to get to know them personally." She believes we communicate too frequently through e-mail, which can be quick and terse, yet not culturally friendly, and it may not translate well into another cultural setting. She makes every effort to meet people face-to-face, to make the investment in building relationships across borders through in-person contact. She believes in trying to "walk in other people's shoes" as a way of understanding them and getting them to perform at their peak. DeHaas is a runner, and rather than work out in the hotel gym, she enjoys running in most countries she visits and finds that the exercise is not just a physical but also a cultural experience.

When asked if being a woman made her overseas assignments more difficult and challenging, she recalled a story from when she was a fairly new mother in the 1990s who had to travel to South America to meet with her clients. She recalled the clients' consternation when they discovered she had left a young infant behind. It was something they could not fathom, and they did not think this was something a "good mother" would do. By contrast, today, women's roles have evolved in many markets, and what may have been frowned upon or even taboo for a woman a generation ago is becoming quite acceptable in the business world.

Deloitte LLP and its subsidiaries has won several accolades for creating a workplace culture that provides professionals from different genders, races, and ethnicities with the support and opportunities they need to be successful. Recent recognition includes a top 5 ranking on *Working Mother*'s "Best Companies for Multicultural Women" list and a top 10 ranking on *DiversityInc*'s "Top 50 Best Companies for Diversity" list. Two Deloitte professionals, Cathy Benko and Anne Weissberg, have written about the changing workplace model, and their book, *Mass Career Customization: Aligning the Workplace with Today's Nontraditional Workforce*, has been a *Wall Street Journal* bestseller.

ACCELERATING CURRENT TRANSGLOBAL LEADERSHIP GROWTH AND CAPABILITIES

The third approach to developing global capability is to accelerate the current leadership growth and ensure that appropriate strategies and interventions are employed for transglobal leadership development. The development matrix in Table 8.3 was created by interviewing successful leaders and documenting their experience and growth as they advanced their development across the five behavioral dimensions. The high-order development takes traditional interventions up a notch.

Table 8.3 Transglobal Leadership Development Matrix

Transglobal Leadership Dimension Characteristic	Development Strategy	Positive Behavior	Derailing Behavior	Classical Intervention	High-Order Development
Uncertainty Resilience: Building on Differences and Complexity	Managing global and culturally diverse teams	Empowering teams and letting ideas flow Acknowledging cultural differences	Stifling innovation due to cost, time, or risk factors	Change management Diversity and inclusion training	Deliberately changing the nature of their assignments to ensure they are globally complex
Team Connectivity: Integrating Across Boundaries	Driving connections across borders to achieve business results Managing people across geographies	Adjusting activities to enhance perfor- mance of others	Expecting others to redefine their roles to meet leaders' needs	Adaptation and collaboration Cross-functional projects	Cross-border assignments that present multicultural and diverse team challenges
Pragmatic Flexibility: Adapting to Other Cultures	Forging informal and formal networks of diverse groups Assigning nonlinear complex tasks	Adjusting behavior and values to get job done Showing keen desire to understand unfamiliar cultures and norms	Unwilling to compromise or adapt	Consensus building and action planning Cultural sensitivity training Overseas assignments	Assisting others to uncover their values Helping others assess their culture

(continued on next page)

Table 8.3 Transglobal Leadership Development Matrix *(continued)*

Transglobal Leadership Dimension Characteristic	Development Strategy	Positive Behavior	Derailing Behavior	Classical Intervention	High-Order Development
Perceptive Responsiveness: Acting on Intuition and Fact	Applying real-life case studies as well as simulations to analyze people and situations	Anticipating changing needs of customers Seeking out constructive feedback for self-development	Treating everyone the same Failing to differentiate talent	Coaching and sensitivity training	Experiential events that shape and cultivate cultural sensitivity
Talent Orientation: Achieving Through People	People development and performance management coaching	Personally engaged in talent development and succession planning	Relying mostly on HR to drive people development strategies	Assigning to a management role Assigning mentors for growth	Taking personal ownership of talent development rather than relying on HR Strong OD leader who drives this accountability throughout the company

CREATING A NURTURING AND SUSTAINING
MULTICULTURAL GLOBAL ENVIRONMENT

The fourth and final area in developing transglobal leadership capability revolves around creating a constructive, nurturing, and growth-oriented culture and environment within the corporation. There are many ways to create that environment, such as ensuring people move from different business model assignments. For our purposes, we are going to focus on expatriate assignments. When leaders are sent on international assignments to develop and hone their global and cross-cultural sensitivities, they require support networks that they can rely on during all phases of adjustment, from expatriation through repatriation. When employees move from one country to another in a totally different region of the world, they are taking personal risks related to their careers, their families, and their children's education.

Regardless of their career stage—entry-level manager trainee to senior C-level executive taking on a new role—they will benefit from and be able to address these risks through support and networking on the ground. Companies contract with firms to provide a vast amount of the necessary logistical services; however, it is the adjustment to the new culture and different environment that causes many of the issues. Assignments that generally turn out positive are those for which the company provides support in making adjustments, either through assigned mentors, networking, or on-the-ground leadership connections. The following can serve as a minichecklist to help ensure a smooth global assignment:

- Offer cross-cultural training prior to the start of an assignment and assistance with adaptation to new environment.

- Assign mentors to junior leaders who are not accustomed to a diverse cultural experience, and ask local nationals to provide social and cultural support to all leaders on international assignments.

- Establish reverse mentoring—where a senior expatriate actively seeks out a more junior local leader to provide insights on the culture and environment.

- Conduct periodic informal checks, and maintain constant dialogue to detect any potential issues in adaptation and change management.

- Increase channels of communication, frequency of feedback, coaching, and performance management support.

- Provide a support network to the expatriate's family, and seek feedback from and dialogue with the spouse on adjustment issues. (Black and Gregersen have found that the number one reason for failed international assignments is spouse and/or family cross-cultural adjustment difficulties.[2])

- Assess family members for transglobal leadership dimensions and help create an action plan for acclimation.

- Offer language training (to leader and spouse) if appropriate.

- Provide repatriation management to ensure that the return and reassignment back into the home country are handled well and the international and global experience is leveraged for growth.

DEVELOPING AND HARNESSING TRANSGLOBAL CAPABILITY

What does great transglobal leadership look like at its best? Companies that excel in accelerating their current leadership capacity do the following:

- They select the right leaders for global assignments.

  - They identify leadership gaps and address these prior to a global assignment.

  - They make sure their leaders gain competence in most, if not all, of the five dimensions.

  - They provide ongoing development and coaching and mentoring during and after the assignment.

- They avoid mistakes.

  - They do not send leaders who

    - Have not had experience managing heterogeneous groups.

    - Lack sensitivity in dealing with different types of people and customers.

    - Are dogmatic in approach and see things in only their own way.

    - Are focused only on costs, risks, and the bottom line.

    - Do not perform well on transglobal leadership interviews and assessments.

  - They pay attention to the morale and well-being of the leaders' spouses and children.

  - They do not assume their leaders will self-immerse into a new cultural experience and adjust without intervention.

Too many companies focus on "filling" global positions and spend too much time, energy, and money convincing unwilling candidates to put their name up for a global assignment. Too often it's "all hands on deck" to get candidates over the line. From the candidates' perspective, risk factors are accentuated with the prospect of a global assignment. They tend to agonize particularly over the following:

- Will this be a good move for my career?

- Is this company really committed to growth through global mobility?

- When I return, will I get a good job and recognition for my global experience?

- Will I be in a time warp and be forgotten?

- Will the company support my family? And how difficult will this be for them?

- Will my children's education be impacted?

- Will we adjust socially in the new surroundings?

Companies that have a history of making global assignments successful are those that have spent time anticipating and addressing these questions in advance and creating a highly supportive and networked culture for the assignees. As noted throughout this book, these companies also tend to excel in providing cross-cultural and global mobility opportunities to high-potential talent very early on in their careers. They offer these leaders full support during their assignment through mentoring and coaching, and they focus on their leaders' growth and development during all phases of expatriation and repatriation.

Ways to enhance the global experience for leaders include:

- Communicating the importance of the global experience and its connection to the global strategy

- Celebrating successes, sharing case studies and success stories of other returning expats, and appreciating how the experience enriched their lives and those of their families

- Creating and communicating a vision for the future growth of the company and understanding how global expansion of skills and talent play a key role in advancing that vision

- Building a foundation and culture where global moves become endemic within the organization and people flourish as a result

- Ensuring they report to higher level leaders who exemplify the transglobal behaviors and have a constructive and people-oriented impact on the organization

CONCLUSION

To sum it up, the example that a company sets through its actions is what gets noticed and appreciated and ultimately drives engagement and strength in leadership. Catriona Noble, the current CEO of McDonald's Australia, shared her personal story of alignment and allegiance to the company that evolved as a result of her observation of how deeply supportive and committed it has been toward building and sustaining a transglobal leadership talent pool.

Noble joined the company because she recognized its resolute commitment to people. "The focus on people dates back to Ray Kroc as the founder of McDonald's. Of the values we have today— the seven values—one is that people are at the heart of what we do, and that was one of Ray's beliefs." As she researched the best companies to work for, she found several examples of talented Australian staff at McDonald's who were assessed early in their careers and sent on overseas assignments. The perfect example was

Charlie Bell, who started working at a McDonald's restaurant in Sydney at the age of 15. Bell ultimately rose through the ranks and became CEO of the global company. Noble said, "It has traditionally been unusual for a non-American to run an iconic U.S. company. Charlie Bell was identified early in his career, and it was quite deliberate and forward thinking of McDonald's to give him opportunities to work in different countries and with different cultures."

For Charlie Bell, McDonald's (1) assessed and recognized his global talent early, (2) developed his potential as a future leader, (3) accelerated his leadership capacity, and (4) provided a nurturing and supporting environment, thereby completing the cycle of developing global capability.

The next chapter will take you through another assessment process that will further help in the development of transglobal leaders.

CHAPTER 9

Are You a Transglobal Leader?

Understanding your strengths and areas for improvement is essential for any leader to grow. I never shied away from feedback and always expect the leaders in my organization to seek out feedback and take action. Using assessments is a powerful tool in one's personal development journey.

—STEVE BENNETT, FORMER CEO, INTUIT; AND CHAIRMAN OF THE BOARD, SYMANTEC

G iven that you bought or borrowed this book, you are probably interested in transglobal leadership, getting ready for an assignment with international or worldwide responsibilities, and/or thinking about how you might prepare yourself (or a colleague) for such an assignment. If so, one of the first things you should do is to address the question as to whether you currently think and behave like a transglobal leader. After doing so, and if you conclude that some self-development work is appropriate, you should begin identifying and practicing the relevant behaviors.

As noted at the end of the first chapter and highlighted by Steve Bennett's quote above, one of the most practical ways to get answers to these questions and get some direction is to use our survey to assess your own preparedness and then later request feedback from others. To get things started, we asked you in Chapter 1 to answer just a few questions from our Transglobal Leadership Survey before reading about our study and the research findings. If you answered the questions as honestly as possible and resisted just providing the "right" answers, the results of the survey should be quite useful to you.

If you revisited the survey and your responses prior to getting to this chapter, you most likely noticed that the 10 items presented in Chapter 1 are organized in terms of the five dimensions of transglobal leadership as shown in Table 9.1. In the table, average self-report scores are provided for each item, and to facilitate comparisons, you can transfer your responses from the survey you completed to the table below. If you used the survey to describe someone else, please skip to Table 9.2, which presents average scores for the leaders in our sample as described by others. In either case, you should keep in mind that you are comparing yourself (or the leader you've described) to a relatively small elite sample of leaders. The average scores for a sample of leaders in global positions, selected randomly rather than in consideration of their success, would be different.

Table 9.1 Transglobal Leadership Survey: Self-Report Results

Uncertainty Resilience: Building on Differences and Complexity

	1	2	3	4	5	6	7	
Seek out projects and assignments that are new and different.	1		**1.91**	4	5	6	7	Seek out projects and assignments that are familiar and comfortable.
Respond to diverse and subtle expressions of disagreement.	1		**2.73**	4	5	6	7	Assume agreement unless others differ in a direct and overt manner.

Team Connectivity: Integrating Across Boundaries

	1	2	3	4	5	6	7	
Stay detached and focus on accomplishing the task.	1	2	3	**3.90**	5	6	7	**Show compassion even if it jeopardizes the task at hand.**
Adjust activities to enhance the performance of others.	1	**2.39**		4	5	6	7	Design activities to maximize own personal performance.

Pragmatic Flexibility: Adapting to Other Cultures

	1	2	3	4	5	6	7	
Emphasize rules, formal procedures, and how things are supposed to work.	1	2	3	4	**5.20**	6	7	**Emphasize norms, the informal network, and how things really get done.**
Take budgets seriously and live within the constraints they impose.	1	2	3	**4.26**		6	7	**Work with and adjust budgets in response to current business dynamics.**

Perceptive Responsiveness: Acting on Intuition and Fact

	1	2	3	4	5	6	7	
Assume local concerns and values can adjust to corporate policies.	1	2	3	4	**4.95**	6	7	**Assume corporate policies can adjust to local (country-specific) concerns.**
Anticipate the changing needs of customers.	1	**2.51**		4	5	6	7	Identify customers' needs on the basis of their current buying habits.

Talent Orientation: Achieving Through People

	1	2	3	4	5	6	7	
Provide others with specific feedback on their performance on a regular basis.	1	**2.45**		4	5	6	7	Provide others with feedback infrequently or only during formal review.
Use people and human resources development as strategic levers.	1	**2.44**		4	5	6	7	Use technology and process as strategic levers.

Note: The transglobal behaviors are in bold.

Source: Adapted from the Transglobal Leadership Survey—Quantum Edition with permission. Copyright 2010 by Human Synergistics International. All rights reserved.

Table 9.2 Transglobal Leadership Survey: Descriptions-by-Others Results

Uncertainty Resilience: Building on Differences and Complexity

	1	2	3	4	5	6	7	
Seek out projects and assignments that are new and different.		**2.19**						Seek out projects and assignments that are familiar and comfortable.
Respond to diverse and subtle expressions of disagreement.			**3.45**					Assume agreement unless others differ in a direct and overt manner.

Team Connectivity: Integrating Across Boundaries

	1	2	3	4	5	6	7	
Stay detached and focus on accomplishing the task.			**3.42**					Show compassion even if it jeopardizes the task at hand.
Adjust activities to enhance the performance of others.			**3.09**					Design activities to maximize own personal performance.

Pragmatic Flexibility: Adapting to Other Cultures

	1	2	3	4	5	6	7	
Emphasize rules, formal procedures, and how things are supposed to work.					**4.52**			Emphasize norms, the informal network, and how things really get done.
Take budgets seriously and live within the constraints they impose.				**3.56**				Work with and adjust budgets in response to current business dynamics.

Perceptive Responsiveness: Acting on Intuition and Fact

	1	2	3	4	5	6	7	
Assume local concerns and values can adjust to corporate policies.					**4.39**			Assume corporate policies can adjust to local (country-specific) concerns.
Anticipate the changing needs of customers.			**2.90**					Identify customers' needs on the basis of their current buying habits.

Talent Orientation: Achieving Through People

	1	2	3	4	5	6	7	
Provide others with specific feedback on their performance on a regular basis.		**2.76**						Provide others with feedback infrequently or only during formal review.
Use people and human resources development as strategic levers.			**3.27**					Use technology and process as strategic levers.

Note: The transglobal behaviors are in bold.

A review of Tables 9.1 and 9.2 indicates that the self-reports by the leaders are somewhat more positive and "generous" than those by the others who described them. Thus, though only about half of our leaders were described by another person, the data suggest that self-report scores should be compared to a different and higher standard than descriptions-by-others scores. And, though the trends are the same, this also suggests and confirms that leaders would benefit from feedback from others on surveys of this type.

For each set of statements, the transglobal behavior is noted by bold type. Some of these behaviors, like the first one listed—"Seek out projects and assignments that are new and different"—are strongly characteristic of transglobal leaders. Other behaviors, such as "Show compassion even if it jeopardizes the task at hand," are used in moderation by transglobal leaders along with the opposing behaviors. In all cases, however, the behavior in bold is related to global as opposed to local leadership and/or to creating a constructive rather than defensive culture.

We'll use an item from the self-report Table 9.1 as an example. If you're more likely than the leaders in our sample to "Stay detached and focus on accomplishing the task," you may want to make a greater effort to support people when it seems appropriate—even when doing so might initially interfere with task accomplishment. This focus on individual members and the team (as opposed to oneself and immediate task performance) apparently makes a statement that reverberates in a positive way with people across the world. By doing so, leaders not only serve as constructive and people-oriented role models but also reduce passive and aggressive reactions on the part of people around them.

However, more drastic behavioral change may be required if you "Seek out projects and assignments that are familiar and comfortable" or "Emphasize rules, formal procedures, and how things are supposed to work." Others view leaders who do these things as creating the wrong type of culture for global organizations. For example, those who emphasize rules are viewed as local leaders and create a more passive and aggressive than constructive culture. A major difference between your score and the mean score on such items indicates a primary target for change and development if in fact you truly want to perform well in a global context. Similarly, if you used the survey to describe other people, they would benefit from a discussion and advice around "gaps" on these items. You might well be able to identify behaviors that are interfering with the leaders' efforts in a global position and provide them with suggestions for redirecting those behaviors. Such suggestions could become part of a formal or informal plan for personal and leadership development.

As you can see from our earlier discussions, there are many ways to begin the journey of "upping the game" of the global talent equation. Many best practices and examples have already been shared throughout the book. This first part of the final chapter was designed to help you reflect on your answers to the abbreviated Transglobal Leadership Survey that we hope you took before you jumped into the detail of the book. The objective was to show how your answers (whether you took the survey describing yourself or someone you were considering for a global role) compared to those of our initial respondents. This step can clearly help you create a personal coaching plan for yourself or the individual you described and provide a baseline against which to track improvement and show real tangible progress in achieving high performance in the area of transglobal behavior and acumen. This step alone is not enough, however, to begin to transform your organization's talent capability in the global arena and build a global mindset to do so. You must have a broader strategy that guides how you develop your talent worldwide.

Thus, we conclude with the steps we suggest you take if you are serious about being a truly global powerhouse for years to come. If you follow these steps, we believe your organization will excel in the global quest for talent. You will be recognized as a corporation that is a world citizen and achieves excellence at the leadership level no matter where in the world your company does business.

STEPS FOR ACHIEVING TRANSGLOBAL LEADERSHIP CAPABILITY: THE RECIPE FOR SUCCESS

As any good organization development professional or change strategist knows, you must have a clear understanding of where you are today. This means an honest assessment of your strengths and gaps at the organizational, team, and individual talent levels. This assessment cannot be what you wish to have as a global organization. Rather, it must be a thorough and clear view of your organization's current reality as discussed in Chapters 7 and 8.

To recap: Does your structure allow for diverse global talent at all levels? Are you organized to effectively tap into global markets and allow global talent to achieve bigger and more important roles within the company? Do you distribute decision making to do the same? Do you have a clear understanding of the capability of your global talent at the senior, middle, and entry levels of your organization?

You must establish your baseline to define your strategy and to be able to effectively and consistently measure tangible improvement over time. The assessment would require the following analyses and data:

- Critically reviewing the appropriateness of your organization's structure for global talent and decision-making speed and flexibility.

- Understanding the behaviors and skills of your current talent. Using the full Transglobal Leadership Survey as a guide, what behaviors do your leaders in expatriate roles currently exhibit?

  - How do they stack up against our leaders on the Transglobal Leadership Survey?

  - Are there consistent themes and gaps across the group that need to be addressed?

- Which gaps are most prevalent and in what areas (for example, geographical or functional)?

- What are the individual gaps, and how difficult is it to close these gaps?

- Do you have a profile of what your best transglobal leaders look like?

• Assessing the success rates of your current transglobal leaders in areas such as business goal achievement and performance metrics, employee turnover, and employee engagement scores.

• Determining the behavior and skills for the potential successors to the current expatriates.

- What are their gaps and development areas?

- Do you have a pool of talent either in the local country or in other geographical areas who can effectively take on these roles?

• Determining what your global talent pipeline looks like.

- Do you have a tranche of high-potential talent that is being prepared for bigger global roles?

- What are the behavioral gaps that they need to close, and what are you currently doing to close them?

• Creating a thorough review of your current status with respect to global talent to define the true reality (including the mix of global versus local leadership you need to effectively execute your business strategy).

• Establishing focused development activities to close the transglobal leadership gaps.

- Developing a vision, strategy, goals, and measures for what you are going to do to close the gaps.

- Tracking progress, milestones, and improvements at the organization, team, and individual levels relative to global talent.

Be sure that you have done this assessment using the full Transglobal Leadership Survey that is available on www .transglobal-leadership.com and that you have collected appropriate data and hard facts from your organization reviews. Without real facts and measurements based on concrete data, your plans will be flawed, subject to challenge, and unlikely to yield results that will effect true business and talent improvements.

BEST PRACTICES TO CLOSE THE GAPS

From our observations of and readings on many companies and interviews with their leaders, we offer and summarize some compelling best practices that have emerged from the many stages of our journey. Some of these have already been discussed earlier but are recapped here for your quick reference.

On the Development Front

- Ensure that your organization has a cadre of senior leaders that can move and work anywhere in the world. These leaders become the global citizens that you have nurtured and who can nurture their successors.

  - The size of this pool will depend on your company size and your strategy.

  - This talent should be readily available for global assignments across functional divisions and not necessarily be tied to specific business units.

- They should report directly to the top leadership and understand the full breadth of the company and how to function anywhere.

- Manage and move them frequently, and ensure that they develop a local successor and a local team of professionals.

- Expect and reward this cadre of transglobal leaders to identify and mentor the next crop of leaders.

- Sponsor attractive leadership development programs that allow leaders to practice and learn the transglobal behaviors they need to acquire so they can learn them in a safe environment.

- Facilitate the creation of personal action plans for individual transglobal leaders, and review and measure the targets specified in the plans on a quarterly and annual basis to see improvement.

- Provide opportunities for coaching and mentoring as well as reverse mentoring where younger talent from various geographies and cultures can work and advise higher level leaders around the cultural nuances of the region.

- Bring in groups of global customers for candid discussions and shared learning experiences relative to how your organization and theirs can more effectively do business together.

- Take learning teams to different geographies to meet with local leaders of governments, universities, and communities to understand how business is done in the region or area. Have these teams reflect on the lessons learned and share their insights about how they would do business in specific regions, countries, or areas within countries.

- Deploy emerging talent and transglobal leaders to disaster area projects and to support local initiatives.

- Arrange visits to the local schools, talk to the children about their hopes and dreams, and afterward have the leaders and aspiring leaders discuss what they learned and how the learning changed them and their thinking.

- Create development experiences that take people out of their comfort zone by sending them on UNICEF projects, community improvement projects, and public works initiatives in developing countries.

- Have leaders teach in local universities and live with a local family during part of their stay.

- Provide case studies of the lessons learned and the challenges faced so that these can be discussed by and reflected on by leaders.

At the Organization Level

- Maintain a consistent focus on the issue of global talent, develop and communicate regularly on the progress and quality of talent, and make global assignments something that talented people aspire to. Ensure that global assignments are seen as career enhancers rather than as career minefields or graveyards.

- Create clear, simple, and consistent values for the organization so that all employees—no matter where they are—can embrace and understand what is expected to emulate these values. Facilitate communication, and conduct buzz groups around the world so that talent can discuss together what the values look like in action in their environment and how to define them, measure them, and explain them to others.

- Create overarching frameworks and a constructive organizational culture that guide rather than control the actions of talented and motivated people. The culture and embedded frameworks help guide behavior and allow for local adaptation and innovation while they maintain the identity of the organization.

- Consider requiring your senior-most leaders to be ambassadors for certain emerging markets.

- Ensure that members at all levels and in all locations understand your existing culture and that your culture values and embraces talent development and diversity. If your culture falls short in this area, make the needed improvements a key part of your organization's strategy and cultural development initiatives.

- Measure and celebrate success through customer and employee case studies and stories.

CONCLUSION

Based on our interviews and readings, those are just a few of the things that your organization can do; it is certain that there are many more. We have hit some of the more fundamental approaches here and in the case studies and quotes presented in previous chapters. Above all, the most important strategy is to get personally involved in making your team and yourself true transglobal leaders! Get your transglobal leaders together, and ask them to share innovative approaches that would have helped them advance and that will help their successors succeed in the global world. Most importantly, enjoy the journey!

Bon voyage!
有個美好且成功的旅程!

Turvallista matkaa!

Buen viaje!

Счастливого пути!

सुरक्षित यात्रा

biztonságos utazás

**Go to the full transglobal leadership survey
at www.transglobal-leadership.com.**

Notes

CHAPTER 2

1. J. Stewart Black and Hal B. Gergersen, *It Starts with One: Changing Individuals Changes Organizations,* Pearson Education/Prentice Hall, Upper Saddle River, NJ, 2008.
2. Malcolm Gladwell, *Outliers: The Story of Success,* 1st ed., Little, Brown, New York, 2008.
3. Steven Levy, *In the Plex: How Google Thinks, Works, and Shapes Our Lives,* Simon and Schuster, New York, 2011.

CHAPTER 3

1. Ng Kok-Yee and P. Christopher Earley, "Culture + Intelligence: Old Constructs, New Frontiers," *Group & Organization Management,* vol. 31, no. 1, February 2006, pp. 4–19.
2. John D. Mayer and Peter Salovey, "What Is Emotional Intelligence?" In Peter Salovey and David J. Sluyter, eds., *Emotional Development and Emotional Intelligence: Educational Implications,* BasicBooks, New York, 1997, pp. 3–31.
3. Robert J. Sternberg, *Successful Intelligence: How Practical and Creative Intelligence Determine Success in Life,* Simon & Schuster, New York, 1996.
4. Daniel Goleman, *Emotional Intelligence: Why It Can Matter More Than IQ,* 10th anniversary edition, Bantam, New York, 2006.
5. Bradford D. Smart, *Topgrading: How Leading Companies Win by Hiring, Coaching, and Keeping the Best People,* Portfolio Hardcover, New York, 2005.
6. Justin Menkes, *Executive Intelligence: What All Great Leaders Have,* HarperBusiness, New York, 2005.
7. Malcolm Gladwell, *Outliers: The Story of Success,* Little, Brown, New York, 2008.
8. Peter Cappelli, *Talent on Demand: Managing Talent in an Age of Uncertainty,* Harvard Business School Publishing, Boston, 2008.
9. Jack Welch and John A. Bryne, *Jack: Straight from the Gut,* Warner Books, New York, 2001.
10. Ibid.

11. Gladwell, *Outliers*.
12. Mayer and Salovey, "What Is Emotional Intelligence?"
13. Goleman, *Emotional Intelligence*.
14. Jim Collins and Jerry I. Porras, *Built to Last: Successful Habits of Visionary Companies*, Harper Business, New York, 1997.
15. Dominic Dodd and Ken Favaro, "Managing the Right Tension," *Harvard Business Review*, December 1, 2006.
16. Robert A. Cooke, Leadership/Impact Feedback Report, Plymouth, MI, Human Synergistics International, 1997. See also Robert A. Cooke and Janet L. Szumal, "Using the Organizational Culture Inventory to Understand the Operating Cultures of Organizations." In Neal M. Ashkanasy, Celeste P. M. Wilderom, and Mark F. Peterson, eds., *Handbook of Organizational Culture and Climate*, Sage Publications, Thousand Oaks, CA, 2000.
17. For more about the Baldrige Model, please go to www.baldrige.com/.
18. For more about the McKinsey 7S Framework, please go to en.wikipedia .org/wiki/McKinsey_7S_Framework.
19. P. Christopher Earley and Soon Ang, *Cultural Intelligence: Individual Interactions Across Cultures*, Stanford University Press, Stanford, CA, 2003, p. 9.
20. Geert Hofstede, Gert Jan Hofstede, and Michael Minkov, *Cultures and Organizations: Software for the Mind*, 3rd ed., McGraw-Hill, New York, 2010. Hofstede's definition of culture is "the collective programming of the mind which distinguishes the members of one group or category of people from another." It is important to note that he believes that culture is learned and not inherited. He continues with a brief discussion on the three levels in human mental programming: (a) human nature (universal and inherited); (b) culture (specific to a group or category, and learned); and (c) personality (specific to an individual, and learned and inherited).
21. Earley and Ang, *Cultural Intelligence: Individual Interactions Across Cultures*, p. 9.
22. Ibid., preface, p. xii.
23. Goleman, *Emotional Intelligence*.
24. Ibid.
25. Robert J. House, Paul J. Hanges, Mansour Javidan, Peter W. Dorfman, and Vipin Gupta, *Culture, Leadership, and Organizations: The GLOBE Study of 62 Societies*, Sage Publications, Thousand Oaks, CA, 2004.
26. (a) Albert Bandura, *Self-efficacy: The Exercise of Control*, W.H. Freeman, New York, 1997; (b) Edwin A. Locke and Gary P. Latham, *A Theory of Goal Setting & Task Performance*, Prentice-Hall, NJ, 1990; (c) Tanya L. Chartrand and John Bargh, "The Chameleon Effect: The Perception-

Behavior Link and Social Interaction," *Journal of Personality and Social Psychology*, vol. 76, no. 6, 1999, pp. 893–910; (d) Earley and Ang, *Cultural Intelligence*; and (e) Stella Ting-Toomey, *Communicating Across Cultures*, Guilford Press, New York, 1999.

27. Maxine Dalton, Chris Ernst, Jennifer Deal, and Jean Leslie, *Success for the New Global Manager: How to Work Across Distances, Countries, and Cultures*, Jossey-Bass, San Francisco, 2002.

28. Edelman Trust Barometer (ETB13), StrategyOne, Washington, DC.

29. Doug Lennick and Fred Kiel, *Moral Intelligence: Enhancing Business Performance and Leadership Success*, Pearson/Prentice Hall, Upper Saddle River, NJ, 2007.

30. Jon M. Hunstman, *Winners Never Cheat: Everyday Values We Learned as Children (But May Have Forgotten)*, Wharton School Publishing, Pearson Education, Upper Saddle River, NJ, 2005, p. 76.

31. Stephen Covey, "Unusual Principles," Executive Excellence, Provo, UT, May 1, 2000.

CHAPTER 4

1. http://en.wikiquote.org/wiki/Henri_Poincar%C3%A9. Accessed September 13, 2011.

2. Schon Beechler and Mansour Javidan, "Leading with a Global Mindset." In Mansour Javidan, Richard M. Steers, and Michael A. Hitt, eds., *The Global Mindset, Advances in International Management, vol. 19*, Emerald Group Publishing Limited, Bingley, United Kingdom, 2007, pp. 131–169.

3. Geert Hofstede, *Culture's Consequences: Comparing Values, Behaviors, Institutions, and Organizations Across Nations*, 2nd ed., Sage Publications, Thousand Oaks, CA, 2001.

4. Edward T. Hall, *The Silent Language*, Anchor Books, New York, 1990; and *The Hidden Dimension*, Anchor Books, New York, 1966.

5. Charles Hampden-Turner and Fons Trompenaars, *Riding the Waves of Culture*, 2nd ed., McGraw-Hill, New York, 1997.

6. Robert J. House, Paul J. Hanges, Mansour Javidan, Peter W. Dorfman, and Vipin Gupta, *Culture, Leadership, and Organizations: The GLOBE Study of 62 Societies*, Sage Publications, Thousand Oaks, CA, 2004.

7. Terri Morrison, Wayne A. Conaway, and George A. Borden, *Kiss, Bow, or Shake Hands: How to Do Business in Sixty Countries*, 2nd ed., Adams Media, Avon, MA, 2006.

8. Daniel Goleman, *Emotional Intelligence: Why It Can Matter More Than IQ*, Bantam, New York, 1995.

9. Peter Salovey and John D. Mayer, "Emotional Intelligence," *Imagination, Cognition, and Personality,* vol. 9, 1990, pp. 185–211.

10. Christopher Early and Soon Ang, *Cultural Intelligence: Individual Interactions Across Cultures,* Stanford, Palo Alto, CA, 2003.

11. Doug Lennick and Fred Kiel, *Moral Intelligence 2.0,* Pearson Education, Boston, 2011. Also, Arthur Dobrin, *Ethics for Everyone: How to Increase Moral Intelligence,* Wiley, New York, 2002.

12. Ed Cohen, *Leadership Without Borders: Successful Strategies from World-Class Leaders,* Wiley, New York, 2007.

13. Morgan W. McCall, Jr., and George P. Hollenbeck, *Developing Global Executives: The Lessons of International Experience,* Harvard Business School Press, Boston, 2002.

14. Jean Brittain Leslie, Maxine Dalton, Christopher Ernst, and Jennifer Deal, *Managerial Effectiveness in a Global Context,* Center for Creative Leadership, Greensboro, NC, 2002.

15. Paul T. Costa, Jr., and Robert R. McCrae, *Revised NEO Personality Inventory (NEO-PI-R) and NEO Five-Factor Inventory (NEO-FFI) Manual,* Psychological Assessment Resources, Odessa, FL, 1992.

16. J. Clayton Lafferty, *Life Styles Inventory,* Human Synergistics International, Plymouth, MI, 1973.

17. Heather E. P. Cattell and Alan D. Mead, The Sixteen Personality Factor Questionnaire (16PF). In Gregory J. Boyle, Gerald Matthews, and Donald H. Saklofske, eds., *The SAGE Handbook of Personality Theory and Assessment, Volume 2: Personality Measurement and Testing,* Sage Publications, Los Angeles, 2008, pp. 135–178.

18. Floyd Hunter, *Community Power Structure: A Study of Decision Makers,* University of North Carolina Press, Chapel Hill, 1953.

19. Charles E. Osgood, George J. Suci, and Percy Tannenbaum, *The Measurement of Meaning,* University of Illinois Press, Urbana, 1957.

20. Robert A. Cooke, Leadership/Impact, Human Synergistics International, Plymouth, MI, 1996.

CHAPTER 5

1. Margaret J. Wheatley, *Leadership and the New Science: Learning About Organization from an Orderly Universe,* Berrett-Koehler, San Francisco, 1994.

2. Peter Block, *Stewardship: Choosing Service over Self-Interest,* Berrett-Koehler, San Francisco, 1993.

3. Peter Schwartz, *The Art of the Long View: Planning for the Future in an Uncertain World,* Doubleday, New York, 1996.

4. Jack Welch, *Winning,* HarperBusiness, New York, 2005, pp. 97, 99–100.

CHAPTER 6

1. From author interview with David Maister.
2. J. Stewart Black and Hal B. Gergersen, *Starts with One: Changing Individuals Changes Organizations*, Pearson Education/Prentice Hall, Upper Saddle River, NJ, 2008.
3. McKinsey & Company, *Women Matter 2007: Gender Diversity*, and *Female Leadership 2008*.
4. PricewaterhouseCoopers (PwC), *Growth Reimagined: Prospects in Emerging Markets Drive CEO Confidence*, PwC 14th Annual Global CEO Survey, 2011.
5. From author interview with Michael Vavakis.
6. From author interview with Lauralee Martin.
7. Catalyst Research showing linkage between women's representation on boards and the company's bottom-line performance: http://www.catalyst .org/publication/200/the-bottom-line-corporate-performance-and -womens-representation-on-boards.
8. From author interview with Sheila Penrose.
9. Ibid.
10. Ibid.
11. Andrés T. Tapia, *The Inclusion Paradox*, Hewitt Associates, Lincolnshire, IL, 2009, p. 10.
12. J. Stewart Black, PhD, professor at INSEAD, Leading for Results: Making the Best Out of Diverse Teams presentation slides. September 2005. Used with permission.
13. Ibid.
14. From author interview with Clayton Daley.
15. Richard E. Nisbett, *The Geography of Thought*, Free Press/Simon & Schuster, New York, 2003.
16. Tapia, *The Inclusion Paradox*, p. 48.
17. http://diversityinc.com/diversity-events/diversityinc-top-company-for -generational-communications-video/. Accessed December 10, 2011.
18. http://diversityinc.com/diversity-events/diversityinc-top-company-for -working-families-video/. Accessed December 10, 2011.
19. http://diversityinc.com/the-2011-diversityinc-top-50/no-1-kaiser -permanente/. Accessed December 10, 2011.
20. From an author interview with Deb DeHaas of Deloitte LLP. Please see http://www.deloitte.com/us/about for a detailed description of the legal structure of Deloitte LLP and its subsidiaries.
21. From an author interview with Deb DeHaas of Deloitte LLP. Please see http://www.deloitte.com/us/about for a detailed description of the legal structure of Deloitte LLP and its subsidiaries.

22. Patricia Sowell Harris, *None of Us Is as Good as All of Us*, Wiley, Hoboken, NJ, 2009, p. ix.
23. Ibid.
24. From author interview with Sheila Penrose.
25. Tapia, *The Inclusion Paradox.*
26. Jeanne C. Meister and Karie Willyerd, *The 2020 Workplace*, HarperCollins, New York, 2010, p. 44.
27. Ibid. pp. 19 and 20.
28. Ibid.
29. Cartus Corporation, *Global Mobility Policy and Practices Survey: Navigating a Challenging Landscape,* April 2010, http://www.cartus.com/pdfs/Global_Policy_2010.pdf. Accessed December 10, 2011.
30. Ibid.
31. Ibid.
32. Ibid.
33. Ibid.
34. http://barnard.edu/headlines/transcript-and-video-speech-sheryl-sandberg-chief-operating-officer-facebook. Accessed December 10, 2011.
35. Anita Woolley and Thomas Malone, "Defend Your Research: What Makes a Team Smarter? More Women," *Harvard Business Review*, June 2011, pp. 32 and 33.
36. http://www.catalyst.org/publication/200/the-bottom-line-corporate-performance-and-womens-representation-on-boards and http://www.catalyst.org/publication/200/the-bottom-line-corporate-performance-and-womens-representation-on-boards. Accessed December 10, 2011.
37. http://www.europeanpwn.net/index.php?article_id=8. Accessed December 10, 2011.
38. http://eeas.europa.eu/human_rights/docs/report08_en.pdf. Accessed December 10, 2011.
39. Geert Hofstede, *Culture's Consequences: Comparing Values, Behaviors, Institutions, and Organizations Across Nations*, 2nd ed. Sage Publications, Thousand Oaks, CA, 2001, p. 81.

CHAPTER 8

1. Morgan W. McCall, Jr., and George P. Hollenbeck, *Developing Global Executives: The Lessons of International Experience*, Harvard Business School Press, Boston, 2002, p. 172.
2. J. Stewart Black and Hal B. Gregersen, *So You're Going Overseas*, Global Business Publishers, London, p. 29.

About the Authors

Linda D. Sharkey, PhD, is an HR executive and business strategist with extensive experience in Fortune 50 companies. Her areas of focus are coaching and developing leaders and teams as well as driving talent initiatives that support productivity and company growth. She is a founding member of the Marshall Goldsmith Group, which helps successful executives become even more successful through executive assessment, coaching, and leadership development. Linda also leads a network of leading companies on the topic of talent, executive development, and culture change.

Prior to joining the Marshall Goldsmith Group, Linda was chief talent officer and VP of people development for HP and held executive human resources positions at GE. At GE she designed a high-impact leadership development initiative named a best practice by Jack Welch.

Linda is widely published in the area of leadership development, culture change, and executive coaching. Most recently, she has coauthored an acclaimed book on talent development entitled *Optimizing Talent: What Every Leader and Manager Needs to Know to Sustain the Ultimate Workforce.* She is frequently a keynote speaker at company events, Linkage Seminars, *Talent Management Magazine* conferences, the Conference Board, ASTD, and the Organization Development Network. Linda holds her PhD from Benedictine University in Lisle, Illinois. She and her husband Tom live in Saratoga, California.

 **Nazneen Razi, PhD,** has over 25 years' experience leading human resources organizations at national and global firms. Nazneen is currently a senior vice president and chief human resources officer for Health Care Service Corporation (HCSC), the largest customer-owned health insurer in the United States. Prior to joining the HCSC, Nazneen was an executive vice president and chief global human resources officer at Jones Lang LaSalle, a global leader in real estate services and money management. She also served as EVP and chief administrative officer at Comdisco and held various HR leadership roles at CNA Insurance Companies.

Nazneen earned a PhD in organizational development and an MBA from Benedictine University in Lisle, Illinois, where she also served as adjunct faculty for the MBA programs. She holds a master's degree in English literature from Osmania University in India and a bachelor's degree from St. Francis College in India.

Nazneen served as chairman of the board of HRMAC, and she was on the advisory boards of AON Consulting and Menttium Corporation. She currently serves on the boards of the Chicago Sinfonietta and the Chicago Shakespeare Theater.

Nazneen has published numerous articles in journals on transglobal leadership, succession planning, and global HR strategies. She has presented at various conferences, including the Conference Board, Linkage Seminars, Executive Networks, the International Doctoral Consortium in Lyon, France, and the Executives' Club of Chicago.

Nazneen and her husband Sal live in Naperville, Illinois. Her family enjoys traveling, music, literature, and collecting art.

 **Robert A. Cooke, PhD,** is the CEO and director of Human Synergistics International and Associate Professor Emeritus of Management at the University of Illinois at Chicago (UIC). Prior to joining UIC, Rob was an associate research scientist at the University of Michigan's Survey Research Center (Institute for Social Research) and a visiting scholar at Stanford University. He received his PhD in organizational behavior from the Kellogg School of Management, Northwestern University, where he was a National Defense and Commonwealth Edison Fellow.

Rob has developed significant research-based surveys used by consultants and organizations around the world for leadership development, team building, and organizational change. His surveys include the Organizational Culture Inventory, Leadership/Impact, and Group Styles Inventory. Rob has worked extensively with consultants and directly with global organizations and their leaders on change and development initiatives based on these and other surveys published by Human Synergistics.

The author of numerous scholarly articles and chapters, Rob's research has been selected for the William Davis Award for outstanding scholarly research and the Douglas McGregor Memorial Award for Excellence in the Applied Social Sciences. His teaching has been recognized with the MBA Professor of the Year Award and the Alumni Award for Outstanding Teaching at UIC.

Rob and his wife Janet, who is also his coauthor on many surveys and training materials, live in Long Grove, Illinois, and St. Petersburg, Florida.

Peter A. Barge returned home to Australia in July 2010 after 20 years of living and working overseas. During this period he lived in New York and Singapore twice and Chicago once. His most recent assignment was as the CEO of Jones Lang LaSalle's Asia Pacific region, where he oversaw a staff of 18,000 people spread across 60 Asia Pacific offices and 13 countries.

Peter has held CEO and leadership positions in the property, hotel and tourism, and education and technology sectors. He has been able to marry the hard edge needed to manage within a New York–listed public company while still practicing his lifetime interests in meditation as well as permaculture and sustainability.

An author of *The Little Book of Big Decisions* published by Wiley & Sons in May 2005, he was the editor of another Wiley publication: *The Little Book of Real Estate Definitions Asia Pacific*, a tool widely used by real estate professionals across the region. He also authored *The Art of . . .* series (now in its tenth edition) covering hotel services and operations, and he coauthored *International Hospitality Industry Organisational and Operational Issues*.

Peter has served on listed and private company boards in the United Kingdom, Middle East, Singapore, and Australia. He is also a sought-after presenter at high-level business conferences and a facilitator for off-site workshops. He is regularly quoted or seen in Tier 1 media across Asia commenting on emerging Asian real estate trends, tourism, global outsourcing, and cross-cultural leadership and talent management.

Peter is married to writer Kinchem Hegedus, has two children, and spends his time between his permaculture farm in Jamberoo south of Sydney and "The Rift" on the Southern Highlands. Both properties provide a working and private retreat for artists, writers, and trainers, offering offsites in an environmentally friendly and sustainable location.

Index